Bullying
Truth, Myths, and What To Do!

Award Winning Author, Master Instructor
DR. GREG MOODY

Amyi
Gain Knowledge
and understanding, Then
Have courage To Act!
Guen Tim

From Dr. Moody's Events, Seminars and Work:

*Chief Master Greg Moody has always been at the forefront of developing new programs to help people in martial arts. He has been instrumental, both in Arizona and now world-wide in developing marketing and business plans and more recently in the development of a Bullying Prevention program. I have seen first hand, the impact that his Bullying Prevention programs have had on children training at martial arts schools across the country and how martial arts instructors have been able to easily incorporate his programs into their own curriculum. - **Sarah Perry, Associate Professor at University of Massachusetts Amherst***

*Greg is a great leader. He has a great knowledge of marketing and management. He constantly strives to provide the most professional atmosphere possible. I always enjoy working with Greg because of his honesty and willingness to help others reach their full potential. I would recommend Greg as someone to work with or work for. - **Kathy Young, Vice President - Partnering with educators and community leaders to improve the health of the next generation***

*Mr. Moody delivered a well-researched training for my staff of teachers. His presentation was meaningful, personal, and contained many activities to keep us engaged. He is a great presenter, and I would recommend his services to anyone who needs training. - **Jennifer Hinckley, School Psychologist***

We had the pleasure of receiving an "Introduction to Goal Setting Workshop" from Greg Moody. The *presentation was a high level introduction of the importance, process and benefits of goal setting. This included a class exercise with a team discussion that was led by Greg. Feedback from the ten participants was positive and Greg's presentation was well received. - **Jateen Thakkar - Banner Health, Phoenix, AZ***

*I have worked with Greg Moody for over 15 years and find his work ethic and content of knowledge to be second to none. Dr. Moody's knowledge of martial arts, curriculum design, marketing, IT systems, sales, and working with challenged and gifted children allows him to contribute greatly to all projects.The programs that we have developed together are to numerous to mention. Each program however has raised the standards within our industry, therefore allowing our organization to be viewed as the leaders in our industry, and pillars of strength for the communities across the world that we serve. - **Rick Abair, CMCA®, AMS®, Director of Human Resources at SBB Management Company, AAMC***

*I have been taking seminars from Greg Moody for over 20 years and am always impressed with his extensive knowledge. He is very passionate and has the ability to make complex topics easy to comprehend. – **Michelle Lee, Tempe, AZ***

I met Dr. Moody in 2000 whilst enrolling my son into TKD. I had been a student of several other martial arts including MuDukun TKD and was welcome to continue my studies with him. Dr. Moody is an amazing listener, teacher and leader. And he will be part of my thoughts for the rest of my life. Thank you sir... - **Michael Harris, Chief Innovation Officer at GlobalMed Telemedicine**

You expect a martial arts instructor to know martial arts. Few such experts are skilled at teaching. Even fewer have the organizational skills to build an effective, sustainable curriculum. Master Moody leverages his unique combination of all of these skills to provide best-in-class training. My wife, children, and I have studied under Master Moody for eight years and have grown tremendously under his guidance. I highly recommend him and his schools. - **Jerry Grula, Retired -- Technology Sales & Business Development**

Ch. Master Moody knows his stuff! Great examples and easy to use strategies to implement easily and immediately. I highly recommend anything Master Moody teaches. – **Scott Karpiuk, Vancouver, BC, Canada**

I liked that part how to teach Preschool kids, a coach has to do with them also and they must do everything with one coach all the time. This challenged me to start a class of the 3 to 4yrs old. Thank you must Master Moody I wish I can have curriculum for these kids to start soon, I have been turning parents away. – **Keorapetse Mogopodi, Botswana, Africa**

The webinars provided by Master Moody are excellent. The content is clear and concise and has helped me to improve my own teaching methods and to update my team by expanding their knowledge base – **John Robertson**

Bullying
Truth, Myths, and What To Do!

Library of Congress Cataloging-in-Publication Data
Library of Congress Cataloging-in-Publication Data is available upon
request.
ISBN: 9798874138547

Author Website: DrGregMoody.com

Published By: **Rev Publish | Rev Marketing 2U, Inc.**

RevPublish.com

This book is dedicated to the thousands of students I have

had the privilege of working with over these many years.

The greatest gift is the knowledge that they go on to help

others by preventing violence, conflict, and bullying.

Contents:

About the Author
Dr. Greg Moody, Master Instructor

Greg Moody is recognized across the country as one of the nation's top martial arts instructors. He was recognized by the American Taekwondo Association (the largest single style martial arts organization in the world) as the Instructor of the Year in 1999. In addition, he was honored with a Special Service award for developing a special curriculum for pre-school age kids. His schools have been selected the Nation's Number One Schools for eight years in a row—no school has ever earned that honor so many times. He also teaches seminars around the nation on instruction, curriculum, marketing, and business.

Chief Master Moody's experience goes far beyond martial arts. He has a bachelor's degree in engineering from Arizona State University, a Master's Degree in Counseling from ASU's Education college and has a Ph.D. in Curriculum and Instruction with specialization in special education and counseling psychology.

In the education field, he's the national expert on the relationship between bullying and martial arts. He is a certified trainer in the Olweus Bullying Prevention Program

(OBPP). His research showed that martial arts does indeed reduce bullying in kids and further research indicated a link between martial arts training and improved self-esteem in kids. All research prior to this was only survey or case study work—this was the first controlled academic experiment ever done. He is dedicating future research activity to the links between martial arts and their benefits for kids.

He has helped martial arts schools all over the nation. Many schools have doubled or tripled their business success due to coaching and working with Chief Master Moody. This is not just due to business advice, but because of the complete attention to all aspects of running a martial arts academy. He feels everything done in a martial arts school must be with extreme student service, with benefits to the students first in mind. Success in business and in life starts with integrity.

Starting martial arts in 1989, he earned his first-degree black belt in only 20 months and his seventh degree black belt in 2012, the title of Senior Master Instructor in 2013, 8th Degree Black Belt in 2019 and will achieve the title of Chief Master in 2020. He is a certified instructor in all primary weapons system, including single, double weapons, two styles of long staff, three sectional staff, cane, Ssahng Nat (Kama) and more. He also holds certifications in Joint Locks, Knife Defense, Pressure Point Control Tactics, Tai Chi, Ground Fighting, Olympic Sparring, Compliance / Defense / Takedown (CDT), Last Resort Tactics (LRT), Sexual Harassment and Rape Prevention (SHARP), and Keysi Fighting Method (KFM). He is also an Olweus Bullying Prevention Certified Trainer.

Foreword

Dr. Greg Moody has written one of the most insightful books on the subject of Bullying that I have ever read.

He leaves no stone unturned. Dr. Moody addresses all aspects of bullying. He explains the effect of bullying on a child's psyche. He clarifies the definition of bullying, and also addresses the importance of the educational systems improving their understanding of the complexity of Bullying problem.

The book teaches the importance of examining whether an action is really bullying by asking three questions: Was there intention to hurt? Was it repeated over time? Was there an imbalance of power?

Dr. Moody backs up his theories with statistics that are shocking: One in three children are bullied.

This book is a must-read for every parent, school administrator, teacher, and athletic coach.

Parents will learn how to recognize bullying. They will also learn to examine their own actions to see if they are bullying their own child. His martial arts statistics shows how a quality martial arts program that teaches life skills is one of the best ways to teach a child the confidence and courage to stand up to bullies.

Patti Barnum,
8th Degree Black Belt
Chief Master Instructor
Certified Olweus Bullying Prevention Instructor

"It ain't what you don't know that gets you into trouble. It's what you know for sure that just ain't so."

— Mark Twain

Introduction

I started with that Mark Twain quote because in this book you may find out how much your "what we know for sure" may just not be true.

Bullying is the most *common* danger affecting children today. One in three kids are affected by bullying at any given time. Unfortunately, just about all strategies (in elementary schools, churches, and in "common knowledge") do not work and are based on myths and misperceptions that can damage children in severe and profound ways. This book will reveal these very common, damaging myths and show the real research and data that will help parents, educators, and anyone who wants to help kids!

Whenever I talk about bullying to my friends, I get a reaction like, *"Oh yeah, it's great you're doing that! It's important! But for my kids..."* and then a STORY comes next...

The story is always something like this: "All that's well and good, but for my daughters, I taught them to stand up for themselves. If anybody bullied them, they'd know what to do [meaning they'd be able to stand up for themselves and ultimately **fight** them] and nobody bothers them." Another well-known martial artist told me, "Oh it's amazing you're doing that work... I'm really interested. I had a cousin who was bullied and had developmental problems. I told him when the guys at school bothered him to knock their legs out from under them and they wouldn't get bullied anymore! That worked!". He was quite proud of that.

People come out of the proverbial woodwork both praising the work I do and at the same time having an underlying idea that the real thing to do for their kids is to tell them to *"stand up for themselves"*- meaning <u>fight</u> back. Often this involves some form of physically *"knocking them down once and they won't bother you again"*. Ignoring the fact that in school your child is going to get suspended for fighting, and in an adult bullying situation, that's called assault. These stories **miss the point entirely**. If those solutions worked, then **it wasn't bullying in the first place!**

I'd invite you to put yourself in a different situation. Imagine you're the child:

Kevin started bothering you just about every day at school. He's bigger than you. He's in fifth grade, and for some reason, he picked you out, a little third grader. In fact, he's a particularly popular fifth grader with lots of friends. He's great at sports and you are a pretty normal third grader, at least that's how it feels.

He started tripping you on the playground and calling you names. It's not just Kevin now, but all his friends (and some of yours) laugh when it happens. Of course, it's not enough to get the attention of the teachers because it doesn't look like a fight. It happens quickly, and then it's over. There's a lot of other things going on, and while the teachers are watching, they can't see everything.

It's just about every day. Occasionally, it's more than once a day. Kevin, and sometimes the friends, shove you out of line or when they pass you in the hall. Your own friends can't help because they're third graders too. To add insult to injury, they think it's funny too. After all, Kevin IS popular.

It's every day, every time on the playground. And even if it isn't every day, it feels like it's going to be. Every day going to school, you think about Kevin more than having fun at school, more than what you're studying, more than grades...

Okay parent, now tell your child to fight back and stand up. How's that going to work? Have them verbally stand up? Suggest your child fight back physically? Is that going to work? Give them some cool martial arts moves?

This is why these well-intentioned stories that people tell me aren't bullying. As we will learn, they don't understand the difference between bullying, conflict, and violence. The "caveman" suggestions may not be the optimal strategies for resolving conflict either, but that's another book. As we'll see, with bullying there is an **imbalance of power**. It's more like abuse and domestic violence than "kids fighting," and this is true with adult bullying as well. It's more complicated. We have to understand the difference between bullying, conflict, and violence before we can work on any of them.

My interest in this issue came from both sides of my life. When I started researching on the subject, I was completing my doctoral studies at Arizona State University, and, at the same time, I was a Martial Arts school owner and 6th degree Black Belt. I was working with the American

Taekwondo Association on developing a bullying prevention curriculum for fellow martial arts instructors. In a strange twist, when my three years of academic work on kids with autism ground to a halt (that's another story), this topic raised my interest because of the **magnitude** of the *problem of bullying*, and the **magnitude** of the *misconceptions of the issue*.

We are going to look at the public view of bullying and the view of my fellow martial artists who, as you can imagine, see this issue all the time. They had an even more varied idea of the problem and therefore created more myths about the cause. Unfortunately, this resulted in more problematic solutions: *"Well I know you probably don't tell people this, because it's politically incorrect, but I KNOW you should just hit the bully. Then they'll leave you alone. That'll work 100 percent of the time!"* This is a verbatim quote from a **very** prominent martial artist. I imagine you know other people (and let's face it, maybe inside you think this yourself) who feel that this is really the best solution. Truthfully, it's okay if they do feel this way because that's a common idea. What we're going to investigate is what these common myths are and why they won't yield solutions. We'll also provide some solutions that will.

Another thing you need to accept is that bullying, like many things in life, is complex. As such, it requires complex solutions. There are lots of simple solutions-of-the-day that are commonly promoted now, and which are not effective. Beware! If you or your staff listens to a consultant do a one-time lecture, or students watch a video and write nice letters to each other, well I am sorry to tell you that quick solutions like these simply don't work. Fixing the problem requires understanding the issues, being honest about what's really happening, having a great plan, and constantly working towards solutions. Negative behavior is part of being human, and the way to make things better (because it will not be eliminated) is continuous attention to the issue. Complex problems require complex solutions! The good news is we are going to cover them in here.

My goal is that this book can be one step of the many needed to reduce bullying. We want to change the world, and this book will do it.

Oh yeah, and to prepare us for learning things in a different way that we thought... *remember the quote that we all know came from Mark Twain...* it probably didn't come from him.

Let's get started!

Sincerely,

[signature: Greg Moody]

Dr. Greg Moody

Master Instructor

P.S. A note on reading this book. The first part of the book is for everyone (Chapters I-IV). We'll review the facts, myths, and information everyone who wants to help with bullying needs to know. Everyone will get value from these chapters, and I recommend that if you want to fully understand the topic, don't skip them. Chapter V is also for everyone but it's a "training chapter" that can be *adapted* for whatever role you are in – a parent, teacher, professional who works with children, or even if you're interested in adult bullying (say, a manager of a company). Chapter V is designed so you can restructure the strategies for your needs and the situation you are working in. The latter chapters of the book (Chapters VI and later) have specialized information for specific groups like parents, educators, and more. They are designed so you can skip directly to the chapters or sections that apply to you. Of course, you are welcome to read everything, but definitely read the ones designed for you.

If You Need Help:

Check out the *"If You Would Like To Work With Dr. Greg Moody"* section and find some direct options to work with him or get a referral for someone in your area.

Chapter I: Bullying – It's Different

So why do we care about bullying? Isn't this just a problem of "kids being kids" engaging in normal roughhousing that they outgrow? First, there **is** a lot of *conflict* with kids, "roughhousing", arguing (about toys, about who did what, about... everything), tattling, pushing, shoving, yelling, fighting, breaking things, mistakes... it's a really long list! This happens all the time, every day, and it often happens between two or more kids. This is called **conflict**. And even worse, beyond conflict, when someone is in danger of injury or death is what we'd define as **violence**.

That's why it's hard to <u>tell the difference</u> between bullying and conflict, and further still, when it escalates into violence.

It's easy to get confused because the term bullying gets bandied about a lot now, and it's been popularized on television, online, and in all forms of media. We hear so many bad stories about bullying, and frankly, there *should* be a ton of bad stories about bullying because it is, as we're going to learn more about it, a bad thing, but the confusion between what IS and ISN'T bullying is part of the problem that we're going to address – especially for parents and professionals who work with children.

We're also going to talk about why it's so harmful, in surprising ways that you likely don't know. This why the title of the book is *Truths, Myths, and What To Do*. There are a lot of myths about bullying, and what becomes difficult is identifying what conflict is and what bullying is.

Understanding Types of Conflict

The best way to think of these is with the Situation Map below of Violence, Bullying, and Conflict

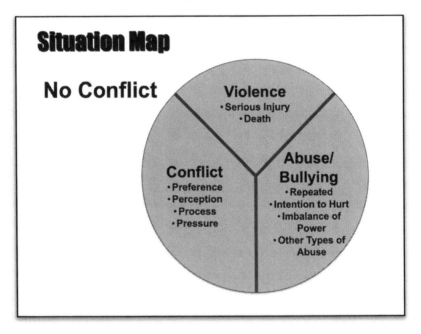

Outside the circle is when there is no conflict — which is <u>most of the time</u>. Inside the circle are three conflict types: violence, abuse (and our specific type of abuse that we'll discuss — bullying), and ordinary conflict. All three are important but *different*.

Violence is when conflict is escalated to the point where there is danger of serious injury or death. Because of this, we always address violence first. If there is danger of permanent physical harm, the strategies in this case would include anything from running/evading the situation, to calling law enforcement or the appropriate authorities, to some sort of self-defense.

Conflict is when people are arguing, fighting, or disagreeing — which can be minor or even *appear* violent. There are four main categories of conflict: preference, perception, pressure, and process problems. It could be conflict about a *difference of opinion* (preference problem), conflict about seeing the same issue from a *different point of view* (perception problem), a difference in how they *communicate* (process problem), and finally, conflict can arise if two (or more) people are under so much *stress* that they just fight about a topic because it's a difficult environment that one or more of them are in (pressure problem). Conflict strategies at a *minimum* require de-escalation (lowering the level of conflict) and in the preferred case a <u>conflict</u> <u>*resolution*</u> strategy with communication and problem solving to gain solutions and agreements between parties. Successful conflict resolution *improves* personal relationships, builds warmth and teamwork (de-escalation doesn't).

Conflict and Violence Strategies are Incompatible

These situations, and the strategies to resolve them, are completely different. If we try to use conflict resolution strategies when someone is threatening serious injury that's likely going to get someone hurt. When someone is threatening you with a knife, it's better to run then to improve your communication. Likewise, if you are arguing with your boss over the best way to manage the budget, it's a really bad idea to punch them in the face (while that may be recommended sometimes with the knife attack).

Now that you understand these differences, as you learn the deep truths about bullying, you'll understand how the rules for bullying are incompatible with violence and conflict. We're not going to get rid of all conflict or violence, just as we're not going to get rid of all bullying. It's important to know that when people are in these different situations, there are different rules to follow to resolve or manage them.

If you've seen kids, you've seen them getting into an argument. You've seen them fight. The problem is it's hard for people for to know the difference and identify bullying.

Why Do We Care About Bullying In Particular?

Why is bullying different and why do we care so much? It's different because if two kids have conflict, they resolve it, they don't resolve it, or maybe an adult helps (in an adult case of conflict maybe your boss or even the court helps). In bullying, it can result in the kid who's bullied having:

- Anxiety (three times more anxiety than kids who aren't bullied)

- Lower academic achievement than kids who aren't bullied

- Depression (four to eight times more than kids who aren't bullied)

- Physical ailments (headaches, they get sick more, sleep problems...)

- Suicidal ideation

- In some cases, kids who are bullied commit suicide (unfortunately, it just takes a quick internet search to find the latest case...)

...And that's a *partial* list. The *problem* is that bullying has different *outcomes* than conflict. Bullying outcomes — because it's a form of abuse — are similar to domestic violence and physical or sexual abuse, and the effects can last through the child's life, affecting their personality, their relationships, their work life, and their mental health — forever!

> **Research:** Long Lasting effects: Teasing kids about their weight = **long-term weight gain!** A study found that teasing kids about their weight (even by well-meaning adults) resulted in long-term weight **gain** as much as 15 years later. (Schvey, et. al., 2019)

We're going to go into the effects of bullying more in Chapter 3, but before that, we need to know **specifically** what bullying is and what it isn't, and how to tell the difference between violence, conflict, and bullying so you can identify them and later know what to do. Be warned: it won't always be easy.

Chapter II: Bullying – How To Identify It

The everyday language around bullying prevention comes from the Olweus Bullying Prevention Program (which is what I will recommend later for all the educators to use) and it is:

"Bullying is when someone repeatedly and on purpose says or does mean or hurtful things to another person who has a hard time defending himself or herself."

This definition contains **three key points** in identifying bullying:

- Aggressive Behavior

- Repeated Over Time

- Imbalance Of Power

Each of these are critical components that distinguish bullying from conflict. In conflict, there may be one or two of these but not all three. Let's go over each of these in more detail.

Aggressive Behavior

These can, of course, cause mental, emotional, or physical damage to the subject of the behavior. Clearly, for us to be having this discussion, the behavior must be aggressive, but embedded in this statement is, for our purposes, that it's **intentional.** There are a lot of behaviors that are mean but unintentional. For example, a kid bumps into another child, knocking them into a table. Perhaps even not apologizing or noticing. This may not have been perceived as aggressive behavior, yet the "victim" may feel bullied or abused. Aggressive behavior can be a bit more subtle. It also needs to be **intended to hurt**. Another example: a child wants a toy, and he or she yells at the other kid to get the toy. This is certainly aggressive, and it was certainly on purpose, *but* it was not intended to hurt. It was intended to get the toy! It was conflict, *but* it wouldn't be considered bullying.

One might say that in conflict, the other party intends to cause hurt. Not necessarily. Often, it's a case of fighting over what each other wants. I'm fighting with you over what I want. I don't *necessarily* intend to hurt you, because I just want what I want. I want it my way. If I want the toothpaste tube rolled up and you want the toothpaste tube flattened out, we might fight over toothpaste logistics! I just want it my way and you want it your way – we have different preferences. That'd be a silly thing to fight over, but people fight over silly things all the time. There's no *intention to hurt*. These examples are instances of conflict, not bullying.

The hurt does not have to be physically hurt. In fact, often it's not. It could be socially hurt, meaning that you lose your status socially, and now you don't have as many friends. It could be an intention to hurt academically or in a work environment. The intention to hurt may be emotionally, mentally, or even financially.

A great exercise, individually or as a group, is to think of five to ten behaviors that may look like aggressive behaviors but are either unintentional or are not really intended to hurt the other person. This can clarify what's conflict and what's not.

Repeated Over Time (Usually)

For bullying to occur, we say it must be repeated over time, although if a single event is severe enough, it can be considered bullying. The reason this is a key point is that often behaviors are small subtle things that are done every day or multiple times a day, and these can add up to severe abuse. For example, a child who is repeatedly excluded at lunchtime and forced to sit alone. Or one who hears *"I'm gonna kill you"* whispered to them every day before third period starts. If we don't include this criterion of repetition in the definition, then some of these behaviors seem minor and may not get the attention they deserve. In these repeated cases, the adults supervising them may not recognize the bullying right away, and in truth, it genuinely may not be severe enough to merit immediate action. On the other hand, if a child is struck or pushed, action needs to be taken right away.

Sometimes these acts could be small. It could be someone bothering another person every day. I'm generally talking about kids here, but remember, this could be for adults as well. It could be somebody at work. If you've watched the movie *Office Space*, you saw bullying going on there. Milton's (played by Stephen Root) boss Bill (played by Gary Cole) kept moving him to worse and worse office conditions until he was finally in the basement. Finally, Bill came down to Milton in Milton's tiny dark, cramped basement office and said, *"Hey Milton, you know what, it'd be great if you could get a can of pesticide and a flashlight and take care of the cockroach problem here."* Needless to say, that was Milton's last straw...

I would repeat the above exercise here in two parts: A) What are five to ten very small bullying behaviors you have seen or could imagine? and B) What are five or so bullying actions that are severe enough to require immediate action? Some could be small and repeated over time.

Imbalance of Power

This is probably the most important key to distinguishing between bullying and conflict. With conflict, two people are arguing, fighting, or want the same things. For example, Johnny and Billy are in a fight. Billy wins. They both get punitive action from the school, and that pretty much ends the issue. Now imagine the case where Johnny and Billy got in that fight, but Johnny *has no friends,* and Billy is the *most popular kid in school.* After they get back to school, what's going to happen to Johnny? Just imagine this scenario yourself before you read any further...

What you might imagine is Johnny being scared to go to school, being scared to face the other kids, the teachers, Billy, and his friends. You might imagine Johnny being too scared to even talk to his parents about the incident. Imagine this for a moment...

What you might also be inclined to say is, *"Well, that's unrealistic. Bullies have low self-esteem, and Billy couldn't be the most popular kid in school."* Here's where you'd be wrong. We will cover some of the reasons and data in later chapters, but **bullies tend to have average or greater than average self-esteem.** They rarely have low self-esteem! They can be the popular kids. In many schools, they are well-liked by other kids and teachers. <u>In fact, bullying can raise the popularity of kids!</u>

You see, the imbalance of power is the crucial component of bullying that differentiates it from conflict. When a child has a lower power position in the relationship, it's easy to be prey for bullying. This is easier to see between adults and kids. Teachers have an imbalance of power over kids. Bosses have an imbalance of power over employees. In the military, a general has an imbalance of power over a sergeant. Parents have an imbalance of power over their children (even though some days it feels the opposite). All these positions **can** be abused. That's not to say they *are* regularly abused, in fact they are not, but if you add imbalance of power with aggressive behavior and repeat it over time, it becomes bullying.

In child environments, there are leaders and followers inside the class and playground, in the soccer field, the football gridiron, and in the church Sunday school. If you observe any of these, you'll see kids at different levels. That's not to say this is bad. Kids *should* be able to lead and follow, switch these roles (in fact the martial arts programs we develop teaches leadership skills!) and grow. Hierarchies are natural and good, however, when there are hierarchies, there are imbalances of power.

As I mentioned earlier, it's a common trope for people to tell the bullied individual, particularly parents telling a child, but not always, to just throw a good punch at the bully. Knock them down, and they'll leave you alone. That's not going to solve the problem, because there would still be an imbalance of power.

Another point that should be mentioned is that the one with the power doesn't have to be bigger and stronger. They could be more socially powerful, have more friends, or have a bigger group. We've seen lots of videos of kids that were smaller than the kid that they were bullying.

Summing it Up

The good news is that you know the three keys to identifying bullying. This will help you identify much of the bullying and conflict incidents as they occur. We're going to help with some strategies on what to do in later parts of this book. There is a little bad news. This comes with a *warning* mentioned in the intro: *it's a complex problem*. You are going to find that some incidents are in a grey area, and it's hard to determine whether it's clearly bullying. In such a case, you will be left to use your best judgment on the right way to handle the situation. When perplexed, always decide on maximizing communication and including the parents of all the children on both sides of the situation.

It's crucial to remember Conflict and Bullying are different and require different solutions and strategies. As you'll see in the next chapters, they happen a *lot*, but now that you know what to look for, they will look vastly different. You can identify the three keys: aggressive, intentional behavior that is (usually) repeated over time and most importantly, an imbalance of power. This will unlock your ability to tell them apart. Now, we move on to myths, truths, and what to do about them!

Chapter III: Bullying – You Have It Wrong!

One of my favorite movies is "A Christmas Story". The hero of the movie, Ralphie Parker, is terrorized by Scut Farkas (yep, it's really Scut) *"and his crummy little toady, Grover Dill."* Many days when he walked back from school, Ralphie (and his friends) would get attacked by Scut. Scut didn't want anything – just to cause the kids pain and to dominate them. Every day they were either scared the attack was coming or there it was! Finally, one day, when Ralphie had a rough afternoon, he had enough and wasn't going to take it anymore. He beat the you-know-what out of Scut (including a lot of bad words) until Scut was bleeding and lying on a pile of fresh Hohman, Indiana, snow until his mom yanked him, still punching away, off Scut.

My reaction when I watched, and I bet yours if you saw it (and if you didn't, you're missing out!), was "Yay for the hero! Scut had it coming, and Ralphie isn't going to get bullied anymore. In fact, Ralphie probably learned a valuable lesson and gained confidence and self-esteem by finally standing up to Scut."

That's what we're supposed to think – that all our kids have to do is "get strong" or "overcome their fears" and that will win the day.

That's why the title of the chapter may sound harsh: "You have it wrong." However, we'll learn that most of us do have it wrong until we learn about it (I was no different – I had it wrong too)! Let's look at the data and find out…

First off, is bullying really a problem anyway? Well, you decide:

- 29.9% of children are involved in bullying[i]

- 16.9% are getting bullied (<u>2 – 3 times a month or more</u>)

- 19.3% bullied others

- Special case: 6.3% bullied others and were bullied – We call these bully-victims, and we will talk more on them later, but they are at very high risk for other issues.

This means that about one in three kids are involved in bullying, *and it's even worse*. To mention a few other studies: The 2017 School Crime Supplement (National Center for Education Statistics and Bureau of Justice) indicates that, nationwide, about 20% of students ages 12 - 18 experienced bullying (so that is even higher), and the

Interpreting Data: If some of these numbers don't seem like they add up. The reason is some research is measuring different data and some data overlaps (for example some kids will report bullying others AND being bullied).

2017 Youth Risk Behavior Surveillance System (Centers for Disease Control and Prevention) indicates that, nationwide, 19% of students in grades 9 – 12 report being bullied on school property in the 12 months preceding the survey. These last two stats show higher bullying rates.

Let me interpret the bulleted statistics above. The survey given to these kids (this was third graders and higher, so they are old enough to be able to self-report) was only counting bullying if they were getting bullied two to three times a month or more. So, it only counted if they were getting **seriously bullied**!

In order to talk further about bullying, we need to really grasp the severity of these numbers. It's crucial to acknowledge how much it happens. Essentially 30% of kids are involved in bullying. That's almost one in three! If you have three children, the numbers tell us that one of them is being bullied, which, as a parent, is shocking to hear, particularly if you are unaware that anything is going on. Sometimes the way a kid is being bullied is difficult to see. Learning about the different kinds of bullying will help you recognize if there is a problem.

Kinds of Bullying

Bullying generally falls into one of two categories.

1. Direct Bullying

2. Indirect Bullying

Direct Bullying is hitting, shoving, or kicking. This is physical content, but it's not limited to acts involving physical contact. Name-calling, degrading comments, and threatening, obscene gestures are also Direct Bullying. These are specific, and you could identify them very easily. It's going to be physical. Think about physical, verbal body movements. If I'm in your face and taunting you, this is

Direct Bullying. You know exactly who is taunting you or threatening you. It's direct.

On the other hand, with Indirect Bullying, you may not know who is bullying you. An example of this is getting someone else to do the bullying. Jack tells his buddy Tom to go over there and shove that kid. While Tom does the shoving, the act was instigated by Jack. It's indirect.

Another example is spreading rumors, telling other people that you'd heard something disparaging about the bullied kid. Back in the eighties and before, if you were thought of as gay, then that was horrible in high school. The results of that rumor were getting abused and taunted. The other kids would spread rumors about your sexual orientation. Spreading rumors about somebody who did something or that somebody's parents were in some way undesirable can be really painful. But that's the intent, to cause hurt.

A third example of Indirect Bullying is social isolation. Often this takes the form of not letting people sit with you. That's pretty classic in movies. There's an IN group, and they won't allow the new kid, or the awkward kid sit at their table. This happens all the time.

Perhaps the most insidious example of Indirect Bullying is cyberbullying. There are many studies that show the effects - one study of 3,767 children from grades six to eight, yielded the following:

- Frequency of Being Cyberbullied: 25% of girls and 11% of boys had been cyberbullied at least once.

- Frequency of Cyberbullying Others:13% of girls and 9% of boys had cyberbullied someone else at least once.

In another meta-analysis, there was about *twice* as much *offline* bullying as online bullying.

Cyberbullying shares the three bullying characteristics: aggressiveness, power imbalance, and repetitiveness but the problem with cyberbullying is that it can be anonymous. You can set up an account on a platform, and it doesn't even have to be in your own name. Since it's anonymous, you can do things that you couldn't normally do. You wouldn't have any risk of being found out, and you wouldn't have any punitive ramifications because it'd be pretty hard to find out who was doing the bullying.

When I was teaching a seminar on bullying way back in 2010, there was a teenager attending the seminar. It was meant for adults, but he happened to be there with his parents. He said that he gotten into big trouble at school and with his parents because his phone was cloned. He had allowed somebody at school to clone his phone, and then they started texting mean messages to other people from his phone number. His school and his parents assumed that he was the one texting these mean and hurtful messages because, of course, they came from his phone number. It took him quite a while to prove that it was somebody else. Cloning a phone is harder now but there are still many anonymous ways to cyberbully.

That leads us right into where bullying happens.

Where Bullying Happens

Based on all of our studies on bullying, we can generate a list of where bullying typically happens. You might be surprised to learn where it happens the most. The number one place that bullying happens is in the classroom, with the teacher present. Now, I don't want you to go be upset at teachers. This is not really their fault. They're not getting training. They're not typically getting a lot of information on when bullying's happening and when it's not. Quite often, as we have discussed above, it looks like conflict. Some kid just argued with another kid, or some kid just taunted another kid. It just looks like conflict. The teachers aren't identifying the imbalance of power or some of these other things that are happening. When we do surveys in schools and do workshops with them, they're very surprised that the number one place is typically in the classroom with the teacher present.

The second place where bullying typically occurs is in the classroom without the teacher present, which doesn't happen as much as when the teacher is present. These numbers are really small, because the teachers are pretty much always present. There's always somebody in the hallways or stairways or on the playground. When it's the playground or athletic fields, where there tends not to be teacher supervision. Teachers are out on the playground, don't get me wrong, but there's always be a dead spot where the teacher can't see behind a tree or around a corner or somewhere there's not as much visibility. Bullying will happen in these areas as well.

The cafeteria is also a prime spot for bullying. There's a sense that normal rules don't apply here because the setting isn't structured. There is little supervision from school staff, and as a result, students don't always feel safe here. When we do a workshop with a school, we'll do a survey, and then we'll figure out where the "hotspots" are. The cafeteria is one of them, as are restrooms, gym, and locker rooms. There's no teacher supervision in those places and no camera. The same is true of the bus stop. These are places where bullying happens, and it's often where there's not as much supervision.

There is teacher supervision in the classroom, but remember, this is where the kids are spending most of their time, and that's where most of bullying happens. Again, don't blame the teachers for this. It's just good to understand that bullying does happen inside the classroom with the teacher present. When we do workshops with the teacher, it's a big revelation when they grasp that imbalance of power difference is when bullying happens. It makes a huge difference in their identification ability and then helps them determine what interventions they take with bullying.

Boys Vs Girls

There are similarities and differences among boys and girls in their experiences of bullying:

Similarities:

- Both boys and girls engage in frequent verbal bullying.

- Girls and boys engage in relational bullying.

- Differences:

- Most studies indicate that boys bully more than girls.

- Boys are more likely to be physically bullied.

- Girls are more likely to be bullied through social exclusion, rumor-spreading, cyberbullying, and sexual comments.

Boys are bullied primarily by boys; girls are bullied by boys and girls.

There are a lot of myths about bullying prevention—what bullying is, what it isn't, and some things that people have misconceptions about. One of the things that we do when we have bullying prevention training is we give teachers and educators tests on what they think bullying prevention is. Even experienced educators have the wrong ideas about what bullying is, who bullies more, who bullies less, what bullying's about.

First, we'll talk about boys versus girls and the difference in data. We often hear that girls bully a ton: Girls bully just as much as boys, and we assume that's the truth. What we find is that boys bully about twice as much as girls. Girls and boys get bullied about the same amount of time, but there are similarities and differences in the way that boys and girls bully.

There tends to be a bit of a freak-out when I say that girls bully less than boys. I hear, "No, no, that happens a lot. Girls are bullying, and you just don't have the right perspective. In our school or in our environment, we see girls bullying just as much." The reason that this is a misperception is, for one, you often see it in movies and in media. The movie Mean Girls is a perfect example of this. There are a lot of portrayals of girls bullying other girls.

To see the other reason for this idea that girls bullying girls is a more common thing, you need to go back to the definition of bullying. Remember, bullying must demonstrate an intention to hurt. It must be repeated over time, and there must be an imbalance of power. So, what happens with girls' bullying, as we'll see in the similarities and differences, is that girls do a lot of relational bullying. They do a lot of bullying by rumors and indirect bullying, which I covered in the last chapter. This can be noticed more. Boys' bullying, on the other hand, is physical and tends to be teasing and taunting.

That can get wrapped into conflict. We assume that when bullying is happening with boys, it's just boys being boys. So, the bullying that we identify with girls, we notice it more. Bullying that happens with boys, we don't notice as much ("boys being boys"). This is related to violence, and this is a separate conversation about suicide, which is not very pleasant for people to think about, especially for suicide regarding children, but boys' suicide rates are approximately four times higher than girls. There are a lot of other reasons and a lot of other mental health issues that go along with that, but unchecked bullying may be related to this. That is just an example of what can happen if bullying goes on too long.

Let's talk about boys versus girls and the similarities and differences in the types of bullying that they might do.

Both frequently engage in verbal bullying and relational bullying. These two things pertain to teasing, calling names, keeping people out, or excluding people from groups. They are very common in boys and girls.

The differences between boys' and girls' bullying show that boys bully more than girls. Boys are more likely to be physically bullied. Boys are bullying with hitting, pushing, and shoving. A lot of other physical bullying can happen beyond what you think of as traditional fighting. It could be kids in the bathroom pushing, shoving, keeping others from entering the bathroom, or holding the door closed so that others can't get out. You may have experienced some of these when you were a kid. Boys do a lot more of this type of physical bullying than girls.

Girls tend to do a lot more bullying through social exclusion and rumor spreading. They tend to do more cyberbullying, and they tend to make more sexual comments. They might say things about how somebody looks or that the bullied girl was with somebody else in a sexual way. Boys aren't interested in that type of bullying. Boys are bullied primarily

> **Bullying vs. Violence:**
> If bullying crosses the line into danger of severe injury or death, this is a completely different category of response, and we must escalate the into police intervention and other types of intensive intervention. This is not bullying; this is an assault and needs to be treated as such.

by other boys, as you might expect. Girls are bullied by both boys and girls. That's how girls get bullied just as much as boys, but boys do about twice as much bullying as girls.

One aspect of this that's very important to address is bullying versus violence. Bullying is intended to hurt, there's an imbalance of power, and it's typically repeated over time usually. If the bullying crosses the line into violence, such as sexual assault or severe physical danger of being hurt or hurting yourself, that's violence. That puts things into an entirely different category. Here, we must escalate the response into police intervention and other types of intensive intervention.

While it may meet some of the same characteristics that we have in these types of situations, sexual violence, requires an immediate escalation. I can't stress enough that this is an entirely different category. If you're an educator, then this needs to go directly to the administration, and then they need to follow their policies for how this is to get reported to law enforcement and protective services. We would not call this bullying. We would call it a crime.

If somebody spreads sexual rumors, says sexual things, or says things about their body or about who they are, or says whom they're doing things with or whom they're doing relational things with, that all would fall into the category of bullying. When it escalates into sexual harassment, the physical touch or touch of a sexual nature, then that moves into the category of violence, and then other actions needs to happen.

It's important to have that distinction. We don't want to treat bullying like conflict, as we mentioned before, and we don't want to treat violence like bullying. When it moves into serious injury or a threat of imminent death, that's violence. In categories where somebody's escalated any action from bullying into violence, then the action that needs to be taken is different as it might cross the line into assault. We would then need to move our response into an assault category.

We need to be really clear about what those are, and it's not always easy. Something might look like one category or another, and we have to be really careful with it. I appreciate the challenge that both educators, parents and people that work with kids especially have in trying to tease out the differences when some of these things might not always be as clear as possible.

Consequences of Bullying

Let's talk a little bit about girls, specifically girls' fears about bullying, because this is really striking. Boys' fears about bullying are very similar, but one piece of data that was done that was relevant was girls' fears about bullying. There was a Harris poll with over 2,000 girls in the 8 – 17-year-old age range.

Girls Fears About Bullying:

→   In Harris poll of 2,279 girls ages 8-17 years

- The biggest fear cited was being teased or made fun of (41% of tweens – kids between 10 and 12)

- Twice as often as natural disasters, terrorist attacks, war

- 15 times as often as dying/death of loved one

- 30 times as often as school grades.

So, a pretty broad poll, pretty high numbers. A very good set of data. This poll was about all fears that girls have in general, and the number one fear was being teased. A shocking 41% of girls were more afraid of that than anything else. They had two times more fear about being teased than being in a natural disaster. They were 15 times more afraid of being teased than facing the death of a loved one.

Parents that are reading, they're not too worried about consequences with you, but they're really worried about being teased, and they're *30 times more afraid about being teased than getting poor grades in school*. Let's think about this data here, and it does apply to boys as well as girls. They're 30 times more worried about being teased when they go to school every day than their grades. *We live an environment where girls are more worried about being humiliated through teasing.*

If you don't think you need to worry about bullying, that statistic should worry you. This is an overriding concern that girls have that swamps out any of the other things you think they should be concerned about when they go to school. A sobering thought when we want school to be about getting academic success and maybe having friends, but they're worried about being teased, maybe having other interactions.

Bullying Is Most Like Abuse

What is bullying like for the person who's being bullied? When we talk about bullying, a lot of times this gets passed over. Here's what adults who don't understand might say about this:

"Well, kids will be kids."

"It's not a big deal."

"Just talk to the other kid."

"Make friends with them."

"They need to get tough!"

"Stand up for yourself!"

"They need to learn how to overcome obstacles."

Well, they could... That's something they could do. For kids that are very confident and have a lot of self-esteem, maybe have done martial arts, and have a Black Belt or maybe who already are in a high-status group at school, or who have some other skill set that would work. In other words, if they *have already built* confidence, they would be able to stand up for themselves. But for many kids who are in this imbalance of power situation, when they experience bullying, what is it like? Here's some of what it's like...

- It's similar to domestic violence, child abuse, sexual harassment.

- It involves: an imbalance of power.

- It's often repeated over time.

- Often, the perpetrator blames the victim for their bad behavior.

- The victim may blame him or herself for the abuse, if it is not stopped.

Bullying is like abuse by peers. If you want to compare it to something in the adult world as far as consequences, it's most like domestic violence, child abuse, or sexual harassment. In other words, what the kid that's being bullied feels and how they are treated because of the imbalance of power is more like abuse than if they were just having an argument with somebody.

So, when you give a kid advice, *"Go talk back to them,"* *"Go stand up for yourself"*, would you yourself do that when a child is being abused by a parent? Would that be good advice? Probably not. Would you do that when somebody's being sexually harassed by someone who's in a position of power over them? If they don't comply, they lose their whole career and their livelihood. Would you tell them to go talk back to that person? Would you tell that to somebody whose spouse was in charge of all the money and the car keys, and they didn't have any family members themselves? And if they didn't comply with what the spouse did, they wouldn't have a house, they wouldn't have their kids, and they'd be out on their rear. Would you tell them they should just talk back to their spouse? Is that the advice you'd give them? Think about that for a moment. When you want to tell a kid, *"You know what you should do, go talk back to those guys."*

If you put it in the context of abuse, they sound the same, don't they? These situations have an imbalance of power. They have repeated abuse over time. They're certainly intended to hurt the bullied person.

The other thing that often happens is **victim blaming**—the *perpetrator blames the victim*. We see this in bullying very frequently. You'll hear the one doing the bullying say, *"Oh, they like this."; "They like it when I tell them what to do!"; "They like it when I push them."*

The victim also often blames themselves. In a bullying situation, they might say something like, *"Well, if I didn't wear those clothes, they wouldn't tease me."* In fact, we see many examples where even the adults are blaming. A principal of a school might say, *"Well, if they didn't wear those clothes, or they didn't walk that way, or they didn't do that thing that they were getting teased about, then they wouldn't get teased."* The result is the victim is blamed and accepts the blame for creating the situation where they're getting bullied.

Bullying is like *peer abuse*. Therefore, if you think about that, what simple advice can be helpful to a kid at school? It may be helpful to compare it to the adult who's getting bullied, the person who's in a work environment and their boss is abusing them or is intending to hurt them or degrading them every day. What are they going to do? Maybe they don't think they can get another job. They need the money. How can they possibly get out of that? It may feel like they're in a Catch-22. If they quit, they don't have a job, so they must put up with what their boss is doing, and the boss may not have any reason to change.

If you advise that person, *"Well, go stand up for yourself, go tell them off! Go to HR."* Maybe HR will go to the boss and say, *"Hey, this guy complained about you."* What's going to happen then? Now they get abused more because the boss is mad that they were yelled at. There are all these scenarios. Environments are not always healthy. Schools are not always healthy. I want to emphasize that this doesn't mean that teachers and principals have poor intentions or do a bad job. Oftentimes they don't have a lot of support or structure for managing these types of situations. It's rare that universities have significant training programs specifically about bullying prevention and even when they do often there is little support at the district level. We've got to be providing different types of support for the kids and for the adults that are being bullied, to make sure that we give them the right support that's going to help them with solutions that will work, as well as support and training for the people we expect to help those being bullied.

Effects Of Bullying

What are the effects of bullying? Short-term and long-term effects of bullying? The short-term effects are as you might expect when you're in an abusive situation. It lowers self-esteem. Self-esteem is based on people feeling like they have a high value internally, and that they are personally capable of many things. They're capable of being a high-value person in the world. But when they're in an abusive environment, they're going to not feel like they're very capable, and that exacerbates the problem. A short list:

Short Term Effects of Bullying

- Lower self-esteem
- Depression & anxiety
- Absenteeism
- Poor academic performance
- Thoughts of suicide
- Illness

If you're working for a boss who's bullying you, you're going to have a lot of trouble feeling like you're capable of getting another job or capable of doing more things, and it's going to have effects on the rest of your life. We see a lot of depression and increased anxiety. For kids, we see absenteeism, lower school achievement, and a big increase in thoughts of suicide. We see adults that are having trouble with this kind of abuse getting sick at a much higher rate. These are the short-term effects.

Long term effects are even more serious. These can affect the bullied for years following the events. Here's a comparison of physical and psychological effects in kids that have been *bullied* and who have *not been bullied* from a study by Fekkes et al., 2004:

Long Term Effects – Bullied vs Not Bullied

- Headache—16% vs 6%

- Sleep problems—42% vs 23%

- Abdominal pain—17% vs 9%

- Feeling tense—20% vs 9%

- Anxiety—28% vs 10%

- Feeling unhappy—23% vs 5%

- Moderate depression—49% vs 16%

- Strong depression—16% vs 2%

When we look at this data it shows the stark difference between a child who has been bullied and who has had a more comfortable environment. Comparing people that are bullied, they have **headaches** about 16% of the time. People that are not bullied, about 6% of the time. *That's close to three to one.* The average person reports that they have **sleep issues** 23% of the time. If you're bullied, the number jumps to 42%. Almost double. The average person, experiences **abdominal pain** only about 9%. That's just occasionally, one in 10 people have a little bit of abdominal pain. In bullied persons, that number is 17%. The average person, also about 9%, **feel tense** once in a while. Those that are bullied experience anxiety 20%.

These are all related. Sometimes you feel a little anxiety, you might have some abdominal pain or tension. Bullied people experience **anxiety** about three times as much, 28%. The average person reports that they **feel unhappy** about 5% of the time. These are kids that they studied, so we're using kids as a number, maybe adults would be a little bit more than that. Kids that are bullied feel unhappy 23%, about five to one.

Here are the big ones that we need to pay attention to, the two depression scale measurements: moderate and strong. If you've ever taken a depression test or filled out a depression scale you may be familiar. You may score higher if you've had a major loss in your life, or a divorce, or a larger problem. Moderate depression is not minor — it can impact daily functioning. This person is sad and may have changes in sleep or appetite (as a short description). Strong or severe depression is a very big deal. This may include very debilitating symptoms, hopelessness, possibly with suicidal ideation or behaviors.

General population numbers show moderate indication of depression, 16% of the time. Bullied people report having moderate depression 49%. That's a big difference. That means for bullied kids *they are moderately depressed half the time!* That's **three times more than average**!

A strong indication of depression occurs in about 2% of the population. Probably about what you'd expect. Most people aren't this level of severe depression. In people that are bullied, it's 16%. To put that in perspective, people that are bullied have **eight times more strong depression**. That is severe depression. These kids, and again, this scale is for kids, are feeling incredibly bad. Consider, when you hear about kids that are bullied committing suicide, and you think, that's a tragedy, it's important to consider that there's a lot of them that are not committing suicide but are still feeling this way. Why? Remember what it's like, the peer abuse.

It's not minor.

Imagine if you went through this in the short-term, what long-term effects might there be? These are some statistics from research done over a long period of time, comparing bullied people to non-bullied people.

When you give advice to kids that they should stand up for themselves, think about everything you've read here so far. The ones that can stand up for themselves probably will. It's not bullying because there isn't an imbalance of power - the ones that can stand up for themselves aren't in this category. They may feel bad, but they may figure it out on their own. It's the ones who can't stand up for themselves that we need to help. Because of these issues, kids who are being bullied are more likely to be engaged in other antisocial, violent, or troubling behavior. They have all kinds of other issues along with this. This type of depression will have some manifested results at the end as well. Let that sit there for a second.

Profile Of Child Who Bullies

It's not just the kids who are bullied that we need to be concerned about. First, who are these kids...

MYTH: Children who bully are outcasts or loners with few social skills.

REALITY: Children who bully are not socially isolated. They have peers who support them and may be known as the "popular kids."

Often, they're the ones that other kids associate with. They're the ones that have, as I said before, popular relationships with other peers, with teachers, and could be popular with the principal, the administration of the school, or in other environments and organizations with churches and different groups that they're in. They may be really well-liked.

Effects On The Children Who Bully

As we'll see, we need to worry about these kids too. Children who bully are more likely to be engaged in other antisocial, violent, or troubling behavior. That are more likely to: (*Olweus, 1993*)

- Get into frequent fights

- Be injured in a fight

- Steal, vandalize property

- Drink alcohol

- Smoke

- Be truant, drop out of school

- Report poorer academic achievement

- Perceive a negative climate at school

- Carry a weapon

- 60% of boys who were bullies in middle school had at least one conviction by the age of 24

- 40% had three or more convictions

- Bullies were 4 times as likely as peers to have multiple convictions.

We've covered what some of the effects of bullying are on kids who are bullied, but now we're going to cover an interesting part of it, which is what are the effects of bullying on the kids who are doing the bullying, the kids who are the bullies. A lot of times people would think, *"Well, who cares about those kids?"*; *"Those guys are jerks!"*; *"Why should we care about them?"* Besides the fact that they make up over 19% of the population, there are a lot of very serious negative effects for these kids. We have to do something about this, not just to punish these kids, but because they too are going to have some negative consequences in their life.

When I'm speaking with a group of people, and I ask, *"Why do you think kids bully?"* usually the first answer inevitably is, *"Kids who bully are kids with low self-esteem."* What we know is that kids who bully are typically <u>not kids who have low self-esteem</u>. But if the kids who bully tend to have average or better-than-average self-esteem, why would this have negative consequences? Let's look at the data.

Kids who bully are more likely to get into fights. That's not a surprise, right? But these fights aren't with other kids. They would potentially be with kids that they are bullying, but they're also with other kids in school. They're getting into altercations with a lot of other people.

They're more likely to get injured. They're more likely to steal and vandalize property. They're more likely to drink alcohol at an early age, and they're more likely to smoke. They're also more likely to drop out of school or be truant. They tend to have low academic achievement, poor grades. They're more likely to report a negative climate at school. Even though we're going to find that the kids who bully do it for a variety of reasons including improving their social status, they're also more likely to perceive that school is bad, that it's a negative environment for them. They're more likely to bring a weapon to school than the average student, not than the kids who were being bullied but than the average student.

Here's something that will probably blow your mind. In research that was done in 1993, 60% of boys who were bullies in middle school had at least one felony conviction by the age of 24. Felonies are crimes like murder and assault. A felony doesn't mean driving too fast, and it doesn't even mean minor or misdemeanor theft. There's a wide variety of crimes that are considered misdemeanors, and, very frequently, when people go to court, they plead down from a felony to a misdemeanor. So, convicted of a felony means it was serious enough that the perpetrator wasn't able to plead down to a misdemeanor on their first conviction. More than half of kids, 60%, that were in middle school and bullied other kids were convicted of a felony.

Here's another statistic. 40% had three or more convictions by the time they were 24. They were also four times as likely as their peers to have multiple convictions. Looking at this picture, we see kids who bully get into fights, get injured, steal, drink, smoke, drop out of school, have lower academic achievement, and get poorer grades. They perceive a negative climate at school. They are more likely to bring weapons, and 60% of kids who bully in middle school are convicted of felonies. It gets even worse from there.

Kids who bully are a group that we have to pay special attention to partly, of course, because we want to protect the kids who are bullied. But we also need to do something about this to make sure these kids don't have other problems. This is not just to protect the kids who are bullied. This is to protect the kids who are doing the bullying.

We're not trying to be nice to them for the sake of protecting the kid. We're not trying to be nice to them despite their bad behavior. What we're trying to do is understand that this is a problem that needs to be fixed for both kids' sake. It's a problem that needs to be fixed so that both kids have positive futures.

Profile Of Child Who Gets Bullied

What kind of kids get bullied? Generally, the kids who get bullied tend to be quiet and cautious, and they tend to be sensitive. That would make some sense because the one who's doing the bullying would get a reaction. They often have lower-than-average self-confidence or self-esteem. They tend to be physically weaker, and they are also afraid of getting hurt. Another characteristic that we see a lot is that they find it easier to associate with adults. They are, in a lot of cases, the students that the teachers like. Some characteristics:

- Quiet, cautious, and sensitive
- Lack confidence

- Be physically weaker than peers (boys)

- Physically mature earlier (girls)

- Be afraid of getting hurt

- Find it easier to associate with adults than with peers

The kid who gets bullied may have trouble making friends. They may not be comfortable reaching out and having a good support group around them. They may not be as big as other kids. Again, none of these things are necessarily true. Sometimes kids who get bullied might also have some developmental issues. A kid who has a developmental issue and knows he or she might be not as successful in an activity are, of course, a little more cautious about joining in an activity or joining in with friends or a group they don't know.

Special Case – Bully-Victims

There's a special case for those who bully and are bullied. It's a combination of the two, and it's called the bully-victims. They are bullying other kids on a regular basis, and they themselves are getting bullied. This is about 6% of the population of kids. We said earlier about 14% of kids get bullied, and about 19% of kids bully other kids in the previous example. In this case about 6%, now that's added into that total, so it's not an additional 6%. But 6%, so six out of a hundred kids are bully-victims. These kids have the worst situation from both. *This is a special case. They get bullied, and they are bullying other kids.*

- 6% - both bullies and gets bullied
- Has difficulty reading social signals.
- Often is actively disliked by adults, including their teacher.
- May have reading/writing problems.
- May try to bully weaker students.

Often, they're actively disliked by both kids and adults. The teachers don't like these kids because they're always having to deal with them. They're hassling other kids, and they're complaining about getting hassled by other kids. They're getting bullied and being bullies to other kids. They often have developmental issues.

As I mentioned before, they may try to bully weaker students because they're ones that they know they can pick on. Then the other kids, because they're not well-liked, are going to pick on them. Then the other kids in the group like to see them getting picked on because again, they're not well-liked. These kids have poor outcomes, more so than other kids. You imagine all the negative things that we talked about that can happen to the kids who are bullied, like higher levels of depression, higher levels of anxiety, higher levels of headaches, higher levels of physical issues, and all the other issues that happen to kids who bully. They might have higher levels of convictions in felonies. They also have poor academic grades, negative climates at school, tend to be more truant, and tend to have higher levels of absenteeism. If you add all of this up, you can imagine that this is a major problem for these kids in a lot of different ways. Bully-victims have the worst situation from everybody, but they're also the least liked of everybody in all these scenarios.

Most Kids Want to Do Something

Let's move on to what the other kids in the environment want to do. Most of them want to do something. Why isn't bullying taken care of by teachers, and why isn't bullying also kind of self-regulated by the other kids? Why don't the other kids do anything? Do other kids not care? Are they actively uninterested in what's happening when a kid gets bullied? Are they interested? Do they want to help? What's going on with that?

What do you usually do when you see a student being bullied?

- 38% Nothing, because it's none of my business.

- 27% I don't do anything, but I think I should help.

- 35% I try to help him or her.

Let's talk about that a little bit. What about the other kids? What we find with elementary school children is that most of them want to do something, but why aren't they doing anything? Let me share some more statistics on this. 38% of kids figure that it's none of their business. These kids, about a third of the kids, don't really think they should do anything. They should leave well enough alone, and they don't want to get involved. Another third, about 27%, think they should help, but they don't. Why don't they? We'll talk about that in a little bit. Another third of the kids, about 35%, try to help. What we know from this data is that you can roughly think about this as about a third, a third, and a third.

About a third are ambivalent, it's none of their business. About a third think they should help but don't. And about a third do try to help. But that means the majority of them, if you add these two up, 27% and 35%, 62% of kids do think they should do something about it. 62% of the kids don't like bullying. They don't like the bullying to happen, but they're not doing anything about it.

So why aren't they? Why aren't other kids doing something about what they think is a problem? This applies to adults as well. Everything we do in this module and when we're talking about these things would apply to adults too. They generally think they should do something, but they don't. Why not?

Because they don't know what to do. They don't know what to do, or maybe there are some other reasons. Let's talk about those. So, why don't they help? Or why don't they think it's effective? Some of the kids that helped will talk about that. 66% of the kids felt that the staff, the other people around them (and again, adult data is very similar to this) responded poorly.

Why don't children report? Here's some more data in a survey of students about how staff responded to bullying:

- 66% of victims felt that staff responded poorly.

- 6% believed that staff responded very well.

So, if you were a kid and you helped, but you felt that two-thirds of the staff responded poorly, whatever they did, they might have blamed you for the problem, blamed the kid who got bullied for the problem. They might have not done anything about it. They may have ignored you. They may have yelled at you for bringing the problem to their attention, whatever the problem was. And again, we're not blaming teachers for this. They often aren't educated in how to handle such situations.

As we talked about before, they aren't told how to identify the difference between conflict and bullying. They're two different things, and they don't necessarily know which tools to use for either case. Only 6% of the kids interviewed thought that the staff responded well. Imagine that. 66% of the kids thought the staff responded poorly, only 6% thought the staff responded well, and then the difference was just an in-between. That's one reason.

Here is some other information. Another study looked at middle school kids. They asked ninth grade students whether they thought the teachers were interested in helping. The first study that I just mentioned was whether teachers responded well. The second study dealt with the teachers being interested in helping. 35% of the kids thought the teachers were interested. They only thought 25% of the administration and the principals were interested in helping. 44% didn't know, and 21% thought they were not interested. That means about 65% of the students didn't think or didn't know whether or not the teachers were interested in helping.

How about this study of 9th grade students:

- 35% believed their teachers were interested in trying to stop bullying (25% for administrators).

- 44% did not know if their teachers were interested.

- 21% felt teachers were NOT interested.

Think about these two statistics. In one case, about 62% of the time, the kids wanted to help. They either didn't do it, or they did, but they wanted to help in either scenario. This is about two-thirds. In this case, we asked, why don't they help? About two-thirds of the time, they're either not sure or they're pretty sure the teachers may not be very responsive.

What this means is that a lot of times, the kids are helping even in spite of whether or not the teachers are supporting them. In fact, often, the kids are helping when the teachers or the administration may not be supportive of them. The conclusion that we would come to here is the kids are doing their job.

Let me be clear about this: 62% want to help and 65% don't know if they will have support. Those are the opposite numbers. This means the teachers may not help them. These are kids who want help or want to help stop the bullying, and the 65% means that they don't know if the teachers will help them.

These are the opposite statistics. These are not matching, even though the numbers are very close. If we understand this, that means if it was 50-50, then it would mean that the kids, about half the time, want to help. And the teacher, about half the time, want to support them. Maybe that matched up and maybe the kids want to help when they get support from the teachers.

But this is not the case. This means that very much of the time the kids want to help. If the kids wanted to help a hundred percent of the time and the teachers were zero, that means the kids get zero support from the teachers. This means in a lot of the cases, the kids get very little support from the teachers, only about 35% of the time do they get support. That would be the equivalent statistic about how much they get support.

Does that make sense? 62% of the time they want to help. About 35% of the time, they get support. Even then, that's not going to be a one-to-one correspondence. So, no wonder it's a difficult situation in schools.

We don't know if they're looking for support or not. What we know is that they're not *expecting it.* They don't think that it's available. What this means is that these are not correlated. If it was 62% of kids want to help, and they all thought the teachers and administration were supporting, why wouldn't they think that?

The conclusion is that's because they're not being told that the administration and teachers want to support them and when bullying happens, they don't see any evidence that they're getting support or help from the teachers or administrators. Or, if they're bullying other kids themselves, which 19% of them do, then they're not getting stopped. If I'm bullying another kid, and I don't get stopped, then I know it's okay to do. In fact, I get benefits from that because I get more popular at school. I get higher status. Because you get higher status, if you bully another child and nothing happens to you, I'm in a higher power position.

Adults Also Bully Children:

Whether you're a parent or a teacher or someone that works with kids, it's important to know how adults bully children. We do this often without knowing it. So, how do adults bully kids? We all might do this unknowingly, or maybe when I tell you this, you know it, but you just didn't recognize it as bullying. Remember the definition of bullying. It was three things: *intention to hurt, repeated over time*, and an *imbalance of power*. You automatically have an imbalance of power as an adult. There are lots of behaviors that we as adults repeat over time with kids. If you're a teacher, you may have to remind a kid of something a lot. Now the intention to hurt is frequently not the case when we're working with kids, so that wouldn't be bullying but it might be perceived as bullying.

If you're a parent, and you're reminding your kid to take the trash out, and they get upset about it, you didn't have any intention to hurt your kid's feelings that way. However, it could be perceived as such. Therefore, it might have the same emotional reaction with your kids. We must be a little bit careful about how we're perceived.

Quite often, things can unintentionally or intentionally be similar to bullying, where adults bully kids. Let me give you some examples. The use of mean names is something adults do at times just because they've been brought up that way, like if a child is crying and a parent calls them a baby or says, *"Hey, don't be an idiot."*

Kids have reported this in the research. *"They try to make me look stupid"*; *"...make a fool out of me"*; or *"I receive different treatment from other students"*. If one student gets singled out as not performing as well, or they look different, this is common. One of the ways kids can get bullied is that their clothes might be different. They're not dressed as nicely. A teacher unknowingly might say something like, *"Hey, where'd you buy your clothes?" You buy your clothes at Walmart."* Maybe they're ripped or maybe they're not fitting well, and unknowingly or knowingly pointing this out might be perceived as bullying the child.

Sarcasm is another common way, as well as embarrassing someone. Maybe they don't understand new material. Maybe they didn't get the math problem right. You were explaining something then, *"If you listened, you would've heard that."* That's sarcastic and embarrassing at the same time. You wouldn't think that you're being mean,

As a parent, teacher, boss, or leader you might respond that you didn't <u>mean</u> anything hurtful by a certain communication. However, we all have ways we speak that are automatic and perhaps learned from our own childhood that are more hurtful than they need to be. **In this case, you may not realize these communication styles are part of you,** however we can be more mindful about how we express ourselves in a "less automatic" fashion when we are the parent, teacher, boss or leader and we are in a power position.

or you wouldn't normally call that bullying, but it meets the criteria, doesn't it? It's an imbalance of power in that you automatically have that already because you're in a position of power over them. It might be repeated because you might be doing it on a consistent basis.

Perhaps that kid is having trouble. Maybe they have a hearing issue. Maybe they shouldn't be in the back of the room. Maybe there's another reason why they're not listening as well. Maybe they have other issues such as ADHD or a developmental delay. If you really think about it, there might be a different approach to saying that which would also get the kid to pay attention and listen. You might feel like, *"Well, there's no way I can get the kid to listen unless I say something like that."* That may be another conversation to have. But adults do bully kids, and we learn these skills to say these things from our parents and from other sources when we grew up. Regrettably, this is common.

With adult bullying, it's common to use repetition of embarrassing words or somewhat demeaning directions than you even realize when you're trying to get somebody to do something. You may not be aware that you're bullying because perhaps you're frustrated by not getting a result you want - you're human too. Now, you may think *"That's not bullying because there's no 'intention to hurt'* and you'd be right... unless really you are using sarcasm or embarrassment to motivate. Is that really not hurtful? Intentional?

What about these things said by adults to kids:

- "You're a big kid! You should be able to do that!"

- "You're acting like a baby!"

- "You should be ashamed of yourself!"

- "Why can't you be more like your brother?"

Or these said to adults by adults:

- "You're a grown man! Put your big boy pants on!"

- "You're too sensitive."

- "I'm just being honest, I thought you'd appreciate that."

- "Oh, you're actually wearing that? Bold choice"

- "I guess we can't all be as perfect as you!"

I know sarcasm is often thought of as a tool for humor, but it can be overused and end up bullying too. We think things are funny. Sarcasm is funny, and there's other things we say to other people that are funny. It gets a laugh. We think, *"Well, it gets a laugh, so it's okay."* In general, I like a laugh. One of my personal hobbies is stand-up comedy (my son does it too, and he's better at it). I like making people laugh. Mark Twain said the secret to humor is truth and pain. Yet, sometimes when people point out truths, we use sarcasm that is painful, and we're not always aware of the impact of our words.

Sarcasm is a hurtful way to explain something. Especially when you think from a kid's point of view. No one feels good about making mistakes. You mess something up. They're not doing something right. They're not doing the math problem right. In a martial arts case, they're not doing the kick right. They're frustrated with it and using sarcasm wouldn't be appropriate unless we have a lot of rapport with somebody. Then maybe it's fine, and then they enjoy what we're talking about. Maybe or maybe not.

Now if you're an adult teaching an adult, the same thing is true. In fact, I found that adults enjoy that even less. Kids just take it because you have an imbalance of power with them, and they can't object. There's no way for them to accept that your imbalance of power doesn't override them objecting and saying, *"Hey, don't talk to me like that,"* because they're five years old, and how can they complain to you as the teacher, or they're ten years old even, how can they really complain to you as your teacher?

Summary:

Understanding the truths and myths of bullying doesn't mean you can't be an assertive and confident leader. In fact, to be better at preventing bullying and developing successful individuals and cohesive groups, it's a requirement. We're not suggesting to coddle people. A goal for all the kids, students, and adults I work with is to be assertive and confident. Remember those three criteria defining bullying: repeated over time, imbalance of power (which in some cases is automatic like teachers), and intention to hurt. Pay attention to all you've learned about what's true and not true, and the rest of this book will give you the tools on what to do!

Chapter IV: Bullying Prevention – The Education System

Unfortunately, there are many schools in the nation and the world that are not taking the problem of bullying seriously! We're going to be talking about the education system. We don't blame teachers, we don't blame administrators, and we don't blame school districts for what's going on with bullying prevention. It's impossible to reduce bullying down to zero, and nobody should expect that in any kind of school environment. But the reality of the world is that there isn't enough done to prevent bullying in schools. We've seen that in the data that we presented earlier. About one in three kids is affected by bullying, and we saw a lot of detailed statistics. Schools really aren't taking the idea of bullying prevention seriously. Why is that?

Bullying Laws And Guidelines

Well, let's talk a little bit about the laws and rules. Almost every state has laws about bullying prevention. In my state of Arizona, we have the Arizona Revised Statutes that directly address bullying. In almost every state in the

United States and in most countries, there are laws that say schools are supposed to have things set up that speak to bullying prevention. When I go into a school to talk to them about bullying prevention, and I talk to principals, almost all the time, they say, *"Oh, really? We do have laws about bullying?"* I show them the Revised Statutes, and they're pretty surprised.

The reason for the surprise is that there's typically no **enforcement** for schools. There's no part of the state, county, or district verifying that the laws are being followed. Why is that? The driving force for educators in the United States is, of course, the main parameters that they have to abide by which are whether or not the students are reading, writing, and doing all of their academic work at a good enough level. That's understandable. They have so many priorities and so many pressures in the school system that bullying prevention gets pushed down unless it's a high priority. When does it get to be a high priority? Well, unfortunately, it gets to be a high priority when there's a suicide or when there's some other case that is tragic and terrible that happens in the schools. Then the focus becomes suicide or mental health or another issue.

That's what we're trying to prevent at the grassroots level, at the beginning. What we have seen earlier is that depression, anxiety, somatic and physical issues, and mental health issues are happening before these tragic events occur. So, many schools do have bullying prevention programs. We'll talk a little bit about that in this section—which ones are going to work and which ones don't work. Because there's tremendous pressure to act only when a tragic event occurs (so they act fast in response rather than proactively), very frequently schools choose to act with programs that may or may not have any evidence-basis, and there may not be likelihood for success in the future.

Every teacher that I've ever met cares about their students. I want to emphasize that. There is no teacher we have ever met that does not feel like bullying is important and that they need to do something about it. It's a key factor in their students' health, well-being, and academic success. The problem is all the other things that we've been talking about in this book. Teachers and administrators generally are not given enough information and education about how to identify bullying and then what to do about it.

What Schools Do Wrong

Schools are under tremendous pressure to take action on bullying, but they are also under pressure for all sorts of other things like testing, dealing with parents, and oh yeah – teaching! Bullying Prevention is a complex and tough project to undertake – which is why many schools simply do it wrong. Here are some "solutions" that won't work and can make the problem worse:

- Simple, short-term solutions
- "Program du jour" approaches
- Group treatment for children who bully
- Anger management or self-esteem enhancement for children who bully
- Zero-tolerance policies for bullying
- Mediation/conflict resolution to resolve bullying issues
- Selecting inappropriate supplemental materials

Below we'll expand on why each of these types of programs don't work, and we don't want to mention specific programs as they are certainly (we assume) all developed by well-meaning people. However, there is one example we just couldn't resist mentioning to give you an example of how far so-called bullying prevention gets off-track. This guy was selling his services…

Just so we don't get sued for libel, here is what was said about him by Dylan Stableford of Yahoo News for your entertainment:

> "A former tattoo artist who <u>legally changed his name</u> to The Scary Guy is using his persona—and frightening facial ink—to teach schoolkids to stop bullying.
>
> Scary, a Minnesota man formerly known as Earl Kauffman, has become an in-demand

"bully prevention guru." His mission, according to his website, is 'The Total Elimination of Hate, Violence and Prejudice Worldwide.' The 58-year-old changed his name in 1998, when 85 percent of his body was covered in tattoos, according to the Smoking Gun.

According to CNN, which profiled Scary on Sunday, he charges as much as $6,500 for scholastic speaking engagements. For that cash, they get something like this:

Speaking before a packed auditorium of schoolchildren in Austin, Minnesota, he barfs up apples, groans, and rubs his ink-stained belly and intentionally pokes fun at the shortest middle-schooler, the bald PE teacher and the 'geek in the wheelchair.' He explains he's demonstrating classic bullying behavior to make kids aware of the problem.

The entertaining antics are followed up with fist-pumping and a steely look as he delivers his takeaway: 'You travel around on this world, and you put out hate and anger, and you cop an attitude, you'll draw all this into your life wherever you go.'

Scary says he's performed in 19 states and frequently gets international requests. 'Kids love him, and many school officials sing his praises,' CNN said.

Not all of them, though. Kerry Juntunen, a Hermantown, Minnesota, principal, told the network Scary would never be asked back.

Juntunen recounts how Scary, in an attempt to show that handshaking and hugging is harmless, reached out to shake a student's hand and sarcastically said, 'Oh, that's the best sex I've had all day!' to a room full of middle-schoolers.

And, in a strange side note to CNN's report, Scary seems to have some tax issues:

'Before we sat down for an interview [Scary] claimed his charity, KidsVisionHeart, is a nonprofit. ... The truth is KidsVisionHeart lost tax-exempt status nearly two years ago.'

'It probably fell out because I didn't report all of my taxes for the last seven years,' admits Scary.

CNN also learned his for-profit business, VisionHeart, was dissolved in the U.S. so his earnings from past gigs have been going to his bank account tax-free."

OK, I hope you've had enough of *that* example. While I doubt there are many programs that are as outlandish as this one, there are many which sounds really good but I am sure you're learning don't have fundamentally good strategies or results.

Let's look at some great ones and that will help you know what to look for...

Examples of Great School-Based Programs

There are many great programs that are evidence-based which will work in schools. Some that we are familiar with are:

- Office of Special Education Programs (OSEP): Bully Prevention in Positive Behavior Support (BP-PBS)
  - Curriculum based: "stop", "walk" or "talk"
  - Results: lower teacher reported incidence
- International: UNICEF Program
  - Proactive network to suppress bullying
  - Results: abusive behavior reduced by half
- "No Bullying Allowed Here"
  - Curriculum based set of lessons and goals
  - Results: lower student fear of bullying
- Olweus Bullying Prevention Program
  - Systemic culture change in the school environment
  - Five components: school, classroom, individual student, parents and community

- Results: 62% reduction in being bullied, 33% reduction in bullying others (after 8 months)

My favorite is the Olweus Bullying Prevention Program – in the research we have reviewed, it has given the best results. It was created by the late Dan Olweus, a researcher born in Sweden who did extensive research originally in Norway but later across the United States along with Sue Limber and Marlene Snyder of Clemson University.

What Doesn't Work?

So those are some of the programs that will work. What are the strategies that won't work? One thing that doesn't work are simple, short-term solutions. Let's talk about that in some detail. Let me give you some examples. I've heard about all kinds of very simple, short-term solutions. I did some work in the state of Arkansas with their school districts. One of the short-term solutions they tried, and they used their entire annual budget on this, was having Stephen Stills from Crosby, Stills, and Nash come in and do a concert for the entire school district, the Little Rock School District. The concert was about being nice to each other. He did this concert, and they were very positive songs. He talked to them between the songs and told everybody how they should be good to each other. That was it. They did a concert. Then everybody went off on their merry way and expected things to be different.

Well, guess what? No measurable difference (to be fair they didn't even measure the difference.) But we can predict, based on what we know, that feel-good programs, short-term concerts *that they used their entire budget on* do not work for anything related to bullying. We can be assured there was no change. Simple short-term solutions do not work.

There are many bullying prevention programs that schools try "**feel good strategies**" - where someone will come in, and they'll **do a speech**, or the kids will **have a meeting,** or somebody does a **lecture** in front of the class or a **big pep rally**. They'll talk about some positive things, and then they'll leave. There's a lot of crying, and people get very serious about it for a little bit. But there's no real long-term effect. Those kinds of solutions or that kind of program just simply don't work. On the contrary, what will work is a long-term systematized program that's implemented in the schools and has real effects. We'll go into the detail of what those need to be.

Another thing that doesn't work is **group treatment** for kids who bully. This is something that's pretty common and ties in another common misconception about bullying. This idea of bullying is that kids who bully have anger management issues, or they may have low self-esteem. Group treatment then tries to put them together in a program where we're going to help them with anger management or increase their self-esteem. We've learned that kids who bully don't have low self-esteem (it's average or better typically), and they don't necessarily have anger management issues (any more than any other kid). There's no evidence to think that they do. Group treatment and supporting them in these ways actually creates a more effective bully. Therefore, group treatment is then, counter-indicated, all you're doing is setting up a more effective bully. I like to say that what you really might be creating by putting these children in groups is a gang. You're teaming them up with each other!

Another common mistake that's tried is the idea of **zero tolerance**. If a child brings a weapon to school or a child is very violent, of course, a zero-tolerance policy makes sense. There are certain things that should absolutely require zero-tolerance policies. But bullying, when it happens to one in three kids and 19% of kids are bullying, if you have a zero-tolerance policy, what effect would that have? Well, there's going to be one or two effects, one of which is that all 19% of kids that are bullying are going to get sent home, which means you're expelling about 1 in 5 of the child population. That probably would be a little too much.

What else might happen if you had a zero-tolerance policy? The threshold of teachers who will execute the zero-tolerance policy is going to raise. In other words, if reporting a child for bullying results in expulsion, you're going to wait longer to label anything as bullying unless it's very severe, right? The example I like to use is this. If the speed limit is 65 miles an hour and we had a zero-tolerance policy for speeding, and every time somebody was at 66 miles per hour, the police officer arrested them and put them in jail, how many police officers would actually arrest somebody at 66 miles an hour? Probably not too many police officers would pull a lot of people over.

Now would that control the speed limit pretty well? Probably not as many people would speed, but the police officers would have a really tough decision to make. Would I arrest people right at 66 miles an hour? They have zero tolerance, so it's 66 miles an hour. They've got to arrest people. What would end up happening is the threshold for arresting people would go up and up and up. Pretty soon it would be 75 miles an hour, 80 miles an hour. Then at 80, the police officer has to decide, I guess I got to pull you over now and arrest you at 85 miles an hour, and if the penalty is you go to jail for two weeks and it's a felony, well, as soon as the penalty starts going up and up and up, I'm going to wait longer to arrest you. If speeding is a felony, and you're going to go to jail for two years, when would I arrest somebody for that? It might be a hundred miles an hour before the officer would want to pull someone over if they knew that meant the person is going to jail for two years. I'm not going to arrest somebody at 66 miles an hour and they go to jail for two weeks because maybe they weren't paying attention to their speed or their speedometer is a little bit off.

Therefore, what will work is to have a policy where you can implement negative consequences at small instances of bullying. Just like if you speed a little bit in most states, if you're zero to ten miles over, you get a warning or you get a small penalty. It doesn't take a lot of points off your license. Zero-tolerance policies for things that are common can't work. Zero-tolerance policies don't make sense for these things. Zero tolerance doesn't make sense to change ranges of behavior that may vary from small to severe.

You may ask why do schools have zero-tolerance policies? Because it sounds really good. It sounds wonderful and popular. *"We have zero tolerance policies for bullying!!"* That makes you sound super tough, like you're taking a strong stance on bullying. Yet as we can see – it doesn't make any sense and it couldn't work.

Another example of a bullying prevention technique that doesn't work is **mediation**. One of my favorite topics is conflict resolution, but mediation or conflict resolution strategies for bullying issues doesn't work. Conflict is different from bullying. Remember, bullying is an imbalance of power, intention to hurt, and it's repeated over time. If you and I are having an argument, if we just don't like each other, or we are arguing over (if we're kids) maybe over who's using the swing set on the playground. We're just arguing over it. That's not bullying. *That* would require mediation. Who's going to get the swing set first? Who's going to get it second? Who's going to get the resource at the school first? Who was right or wrong about something? That's conflict. That needs mediation.

Bullying means I have a different power position than you. I'm bigger. I'm stronger. I have more status than you. If a teacher tries to help or a parent tries to help by conflict resolution and resolve an issue between by just "talking it out", well, that's never going to work in a bullying case because one kid already has a lot more power. He can just tell the other kid what to do, and they pretty much must comply. They might be bigger, stronger. They have a difference in power.

I'll give you an example of that in an adult situation. Let's say you have a boss and an employee. If they have conflict, who's going to win that conflict? Most of the time it's going to be the boss, because they can just tell the employee what they want in the end. That's not really a conflict or mediation situation if the boss is bullying the employee, if the boss doesn't care about the employee and there is an intention to hurt (remember those three things about bullying. Intention to hurt repeated over time and there's an imbalance of power) means that conflict resolution skills cannot work.

The other thing that is important is selecting inappropriate supplemental materials. What do we mean by this? Inappropriate supplemental materials might be like what I said earlier. Let's say we're going to do a bullying prevention workshop with the kids and most of it is about everybody being nice to each other. Now that's positive. That's a good thing to do in *any* class with kids, after all it's great to talk about why we should be nice to each other. However, it doesn't really address what happens if somebody does bully. They should know what happens, the types of bullying, what to watch out for, what bullying is. If somebody's bullying another kid, what are the consequences? What's the organization's action plan.

Sometimes in an organization or a social group there aren't any consequences. As I mentioned earlier in this book, if I bully somebody else, and there's no consequence, then bullying may have a positive result. Among other things, it might help my social status, or it might help my self-esteem to continue to do it. Inappropriate supplemental materials might not include that kind of full picture of the story. The "Scary Guy" I mentioned earlier is a glaring example of inappropriate supplemental materials. This would be an example of a program that we don't recommend, and as you read this it sounds ridiculous yet, in the context of well-meaning people, these kinds of programs still exist.

Another example of programs that schools and organizations use are "feel-good programs". What I mean by feel-good programs are other programs that are well-intentioned, but they don't have evidence basis for their success. For example, similar to above, the kids might write essays and post around the facility about why they should be kind or nice to each other, but they don't have any real function because they don't have any ongoing characteristics of a successful program.

So why isn't every school and community organization doing solid, evidence-based programs for Bullying Prevention? A true story may illustrate why...

As I mentioned, one program that I really love is the Olweus Bullying Prevention Program. Years ago, one of their main researchers was waiting to be on the *Ellen DeGeneres Show*. She was going to have a talk with Ellen about the real issues in bullying prevention; however, the guest right before her was Madonna. [Yes, <u>that</u> Madonna] Ellen decided to ask Madonna, *"What do you think about bullying?"* Madonna said, *"Well, you know, let me tell you what I think about bullying,"* and she went ahead and talked for the next 20 or 30 minutes, and they didn't have the expert from the Olweus Bullying Prevention Program – who knew all about bullying - come on (and didn't schedule her back).

So instead of having an expert that could really give people information and dispel some of the myths that we've been talking about here, Madonna provided her well-intentioned but at best not researched and at worst misleading opinions. I am 100% confident Madonna truly cares about the problem as she had a history of being bullied when she was in school, and she certainly deserves to say something. She's a smart person, very successful, and further, what she said likely made sense to people. But it ***wasn't the information that people probably needed***. This is an example of why the truths and myths about bullying are difficult to get public, why information gets confused and misunderstood.

What Does Work?

The great news is there are many things that do work as long as you pay attention to the principles discussed. It'll be helpful to list a few evidence-based bullying prevention programs. These are educational programs that work, and there is more than a list here. If your child's school doesn't have one of these on their list, you don't have to quit that school and go somewhere else. There is some research you could do, and I'll give you some characteristics that you can think about or that you can investigate to see if their programs support this. Also, I'll give you some other suggestions about what you can do, because even if your school has some of these programs, a common issue is *fidelity,* that means the degree to which the organization adheres to the principles of the program. If they have 100% *fidelity,* they follow all the protocols. Even if they have 100% fidelity, it's always better if you do additional work with kids to prevent bullying because even the best school-based bullying prevention program can never eliminate bullying completely.

Programs That Work

These are some of the ones that we really like or we've seen in our research that work well. Bullying Prevention in Positive Behavior Support was started by my alma mater, Arizona State University, in a group of different programs that worked with the university. This is reported by teachers as a lower incidence of bullying. Internationally, UNICEF has a good program, one that you've heard about in lots of other ways. This reported abusive behavior down by half. There's also one the government has, No Bullying Allowed. This mainly lowered students' fear of bullying—not so much bullying reduction but lowered their fear of bullying. My favorite one, in which I've done certifications, is the Olweus Bullying Prevention Program named after Dan Olweus, the founder.

Olweus has five important components they work on that should go into any program. These components are the areas the program affects and works to improve the level of bullying from all dimensions. They are how the school operates, in the classroom, the individual student, the parents, and also the involvement of the community. This program reported in one study, a 62% reduction in kids getting bullied. Based on the data, it's the best program there is. It also reported a 33% reduction in kids bullying others. This is after about an eight-month test. Now, this has been done in many, many schools around the world. It started in Norway, but it's widespread across the United States.

What you will find is that schools use different programs, which means there are a lot of different bullying prevention programs out there. These are four of our favorite ones, with the Olweus Bullying Prevention Program probably giving the best results and having the best evidence basis for working in schools.

The "School" and "Kid" Components of Bullying

For maximum results with any program, it does require the school, classroom, student, parents, and the community to work together. What does the School Component mean? What that means is that the school develops a system for implementing negative consequences for bullying. Let's talk about that a little bit more. It's not just the negative consequences for the kid who's bullying. Let's say they're bullying somebody. We'll call that the one who's being bullied. But there's also all the other kids who are involved – the kids that are supporting the bully, the kids who are supporting the bully and start engaging in the bullying when bullying happens. There are kids that are egging on the bullying. It's necessary to include all the other kids involved in bullying but are not actively engaging in bullying.

There are kids that are not involved and don't really want to get involved. There are kids that don't want the bullying to happen but don't do anything about it. Then there are the kids that do help against bullying. They do try to help support the kid who's being bullied. This whole kind of ecosystem of kids that are involved need to be managed with consequences and support (for more details I recommend looking at everything the Olweus Bullying Prevention offers). Teachers will be better able to handle the situation when they are aware of all these roles. All these kids are involved in this whole process when bullying's going on not just the kid who's bullying and the kid who's getting picked on. Only then can we move all the kids one step closer to being one of the kids who helps the victim. These helpers, the ones who are supportive of the kids that are being bullied, is what we want to try to develop more of in a school (or any organization or group).

In summary, a school system must have, as immediately as possible, negative consequences for these kids that are bullying *or that are supporting the bullying*. Then, they need to encourage more of the children who are exhibiting helping behavior, and *at the same time* support the kids that are being bullied. In this way, when bullying occurs, all involved parties have been dealt with appropriately.

What can't happen (but often does) is the kid who gets bullied being told, *"Well, if you weren't wearing those clothes, you wouldn't get bullied."* That's really telling the kid that's getting bullied that it's their fault. Or, *"If you didn't talk so funny, you wouldn't get bullied."* Or, *"If you didn't look so funny, you wouldn't get bullied."* Or, *"If you didn't act that way, you wouldn't get bullied."* Well, that's telling the kid that it's their fault. Very often bullying ends up having blame assigned to the kid who's getting bullied.

When one of these programs that's working well is implemented, the teacher is empowered and educated to identify a bullying situation correctly. They, along with the environment around the kids understand how to manage the child who's bullying and support who's getting bullied, as well as the kids involved. The effect of this is that the overall school discipline and systematic culture in the school environment changes and improves, which helps the students in many other ways too.

The Classroom Component of Bullying

When we speak about bullying it's important to point out here that this book isn't just for teachers but for all who work with kids, including parents, and are interested in bullying. In elementary schools, the classroom is a perfect venue to do regular meetings about once a week to role-play scenarios that may occur and how to diffuse situations, how to ask for help from a teacher, friend, or administrator and how to manage situations that come up. Kids are excellent at providing possible scenarios to practice. At work or in other groups, practicing or talking about scenarios is also a perfect time to role-play, talk and introduce scenarios that can occur. Note these aren't therapy sessions where we discuss current situations that *are happening* – the idea is to preemptively practice situations that may come up but aren't happening yet so skills can be developed without having the stress of the actual situation. For kids it might be:

- "What if someone calls you a bad name?"

- "What if you get excluded at lunch?"

- "What if you saw someone getting excluded on the playground?"

- "What if you noticed someone was getting pushed and they couldn't protect themselves?"

Do kids have an option to talk ask teachers for help? Parents? How should they ask for help (so it doesn't sound like they are just complaining?); What's the difference between tattling and telling?

For adults at work, it may be:

- "What if someone spreads rumors about you?"

- "What if someone physically pushes you?"

- "What do you do if you're getting _____ from your supervisor?"

At work, should every situation be reported to Human Resources? What are the thresholds? What's the best way to do this? When do your managers need to be involved and how? What if they are the ones doing the bullying? Having these definitions clear helps the employee and can give managers clearer guidelines about what their roles are. This is a start only... you can see that work situations can be complex and difficult to resolve.

The Parent Component of Bullying

The parent component is critical as well because the parents then understand what's going on. Then, if their kid was bullying another kid or supporting the bullying or having some negative behavior if the kid gets sent home, the parent knows not to punish the kid incorrectly or do something that might be counterproductive, but also, they're part of this educational process. If their kid's getting bullied, they know how to help support their kid in the right way. If their kid's helping, they know to be positive about what happens in rewarding their kid and reinforcing the good behavior that they've been showing. So, the parents are also part of it. If a situation happens where, for example, a kid's bullying another child, all the kids' parents are going to get called and talked to. But the parents know ahead of time that this is how the process works, and they're not going to be surprised or shocked by this call from the school. They're going to be part of the growth process.

The Community Component of Bullying

The community can be supportive of all the different parts of this process. They might be financially contributing, they might be supported at the different events that the school has, they may be on the school board or the school bullying prevention board that they create and do other things that support the process. Olweus is a great program. If you find somebody that can work with your school in supporting the Olweus Bullying Prevention Program, that's a great system to have in your school.

For all kids, educational programs are important. Some schools will have a really solid program while some schools will have a program that may have some missing pieces or may not have much education at all in terms of bullying prevention. Again, let's not blame the schools for that. They're under so much pressure from all kinds of other areas, we do need to understand that. That means that regardless of what kind of program they have, parents, kids, school, and the whole community, needs to be working on how to prevent bullying in lots of other areas.

What Works...

Think for a moment of the point of view of the child. If you're one of the kids that want to support kids when they're being bullied, maybe you're one of the kids that's getting bullied, or even one of the kids that's bullying other kids... what is your point of view? How does it feel when you're them? That will give you a perspective on what works.

In the real-world, even with the best programs, best research and best fidelity to the programs bullying can't be completely eliminated. Some popular efforts to reduce bullying have very little effect. We also point out the characteristics and programs that do dramatically reduce bullying. Let's look at more detail of another one of those: Martial Arts...

Martial Arts and Bullying Research

We've talked a lot about what to do if your kid's being bullied and how to work with schools and how to help your kid. We've covered that (and will have more) in detail in other parts of this book, but now we're going to talk about one specific thing to do and how to be proactive.

We're going to go over this in a couple of different ways. First, we'll talk about what we know is the most effective program with evidence to back it up. Of course, everybody that's been reading this knows I'm a martial artist, and it may feel like I'm biased. When I started this project, which we'll talk about shortly, we had this question: Does martial arts help kids with all the issues inherent in bullying prevention? Does it help kids keep from getting bullied? We thought that it did.

The "why" or the hypothesis of the causes of "why" martial arts would help is important to delve into. We thought this probably helps them, but not because they would protect themselves in a fight or get in fights all the time and then show that they're the strongest kid on the block. We felt like it would build enough confidence so they wouldn't be in the bullied group, that they would develop personal characteristics so they wouldn't be targeted for bullying. There'd be a lot of characteristics that martial arts is likely to help them with that would keep them from being bullied.

Secondarily I also wanted to see if doing martial arts would reduce the likelihood of them bullying other kids.

Anecdotally there are no reports in the martial arts industry of martial arts students fighting more because they are taking martial arts (despite what popular TV and movie culture like *Karate Kid* and *Cobra Kai* would show) yet I wanted to see if we could measure this. We're going to go over the extensive research that we were able to do and what we found.

What follows is from research that I did with Arizona State University in my doctoral program. I'm proud to say that Senior Master Laura Sanborn was part of it, and many schools across the country participated in the program and part of our process when we built this. I'm going to skip around a little bit, because we've covered a lot of the details that were in the dissertation research.

Research Description

Our goals were to determine whether martial arts influenced bullying, both in preventing bullying and in keeping kids from bullying other kids. We measured bullying behaviors in three different areas, and we had an excellent sample of what was happening in bullying. This is called a quasi-experimental design because in a traditional experimental design you would have a group who got the treatment (doing martial arts) and a control group (who didn't get martial arts) and study the difference over time. This would have been too cumbersome if we wanted results over say a five-year period of time. Luckily, in martial arts we already have groups separated by time...

Those were the beginners (white belts). Then we measured what was going on with the kids in the middle, what we'd call yellow through red belts (depending on the style of martial art), the intermediate students. Then we measured what was happening with the black belts. They'd been in martial arts, not in our martial arts school, but in different martial arts schools across the country. They had been practicing martial arts for three to five years, sometimes six, seven, or even eight years. They had been at least a first-degree black belt or higher. The great part was that this was in 17 different states, at 22 different schools. We also did recruitment at large national tournaments. It was spread even further than that with a wide variety of individual samples across the nation. It was generally suburban middle class, so in the middle of the demographics, which is where we see most bullying. We also see it at very high socioeconomic status, and we see it at low socioeconomic status.

To measure how much bullying was going on the Olweus bullying questionnaire was used, which asked the kids quite a few questions, such as whether they have been bullied, how they were bullied, and whether they bullied other kids. They had to be at least in third grade (so they were able to read, comprehend, and answer). This wasn't the parents telling us anything, this was the kids telling us, and the questions were asked in a variety of ways. It's a great tool that has been revised several different times to get really good data. We looked for a good representation of whether the kids are being bullied. It also has been validated by other observational studies.

Note: Sometimes people do criticize this test. It doesn't give a lot of questions about cyberbullying. The revised version that we did give them does include cyberbullying, so that does get included in what we were testing at that time, even though it was a few years ago when we did this.

We also added an additional questionnaire that asked parents questions. There were 18 additional questions that we came up with on their feelings about martial arts and whether their kids have been bullied. The martial arts program that we did study specifically was a little bit restricted to an American Taekwondo Association Karate for Kids Program which was specifically designed for kids, and it has a lot of life skills built into it.

Parent Reminder: One thing to remember is that if you're a parent looking for something to help your kids, you want to look for a program that has a life skill curriculum built into it that's very serious. This means not just a couple of signs on the wall, but rather one that has life skills components built into the ongoing curriculum. The martial arts schools that we did work with had some consistency in what they do, and they have consistency in the type of martial arts they taught. There are plenty of other schools that are not part of data collection group we worked with that do a fantastic job but have only a little bit of an understanding about the programs we did test this under to get our research data. Still, they do have a full and robust life skill curriculum along with the martial arts program. The kids learn these skills when they do martial arts, and there's some honor, value, and character development along with it. Watch for these characteristics.

Data Notes

Let's look at the data we got because I think it's important to go through. First, 227 kids returned the questionnaire. We sent out way more than this, and we had a pretty good distribution of beginners, intermediates, and adults. The mean age was 11, and we had a representative distribution of girls and boys. This is pretty typical in inter-martial arts programs, with about 35% girls and 65% boys. The formal research question was: Do kids who take martial arts get bullied less than children who just got started? We were measuring kids on entry to martial arts or white belts. Note that on one hand while we weren't measuring kids who were in the general population, we were able to have a very specific starting point to measure against – within a month or two from when they walked in the door of their school versus kids who were black belts, who'd been doing it for a while – generally three years or more (we measured against all black belts so they could be training well past the day they received their first degree black belt). Our guess was that they wouldn't get bullied as much. One thing important to remember is when we're talking about bullying, we're not talking about being bullied once in the last year. It had to be two to three times or more in the past couple of months, so it's happening regularly. That's the minimum that they would've answered the question, *"Yes, I'm being bullied."* If they've been bullied less, they wouldn't have answered the question. They're being bullied. It's not just someone looked at them funny. It's not just that it happened one time. It's being bullied on a regular basis. If you remember our definition of bullying, it's intentional, intended to hurt, there's an imbalance of power and it's repeated. This is repeated bullying.

A lot of the kids haven't been bullied. Quite a few had one to two times, but a good bit of them have been bullied two to three times a week. What's important here is the difference between these. We'll illustrate this a little bit later. This means the beginners, the intermediate, and the advanced. If you look at the difference between the beginners, beginners are being bullied two to three times a month or more. 27% of the beginners are bullied two to three times a month or more. Now if you remember from earlier in the book, the average was 14% for the general population.

This was an important discovery that kids who come to martial arts are being bullied twice as much as the general population. Now let me give you a little bit of a spoiler. When we asked parents the question of whether their kids are being bullied, they answered that *they didn't think their kids were getting bullied this much*. Parents were unaware that this was happening, but kids in their own reports were getting bullied about twice as much as the general population. If you look at the advanced group, the black belts, they were getting bullied about 10% of the time.

> **Key Point: Kids who start martial arts are bullied roughly TWICE as much as the general population... Parents think their kids are bullied much less...**

This comparison was 64% less. Now again, spoiler alert, we're going to go through this, but the best bullying prevention program that we know of, and that's the Olweus Program and the best study in the best circumstances that they had, where they implemented the program really well, that reduced bullying about 60%. This program across the data that we gathered was better than the best school-based bullying prevention program. Putting your kids into martial arts was better than the best school-based bullying prevention program. It reduced bullying more than any other thing that we've measured.

> **Key Point: Getting a Black Belt is more effective than any school-based bullying prevention program. It's one thing parents can control to keep their kids safe from bullying...**

I've been involved with martial arts for so long, and I felt like the parents were bringing the kids in because of bullying, but the data shows that the parents didn't even know that the kids were being bullied. That's an important point. We would notice that because about 14%, isn't a small number. So that means about one to two of every 10 parents would say, *"My kid's getting bullied. We want some help with that."* That's pretty big. That's a major issue that we'd want to help them with. And based on this data, it's probably more severe if the parents are noticing it. Every time you hear one of those stories, there's another kid that's not telling their parents about it, and the parents are unaware that this is going on.

In the case of our research, it was anonymous whether they were getting bullied. We coded the questionnaires. This is important information so that we'd know which parent matched which kid, but the parent and the kid didn't know that. And we didn't know which kid was with which parent. The study was blind in that way, but we could tie the surveys together.

> **Key Point: Parents often don't know their kids are being bullied...**

Other Research Notes

One other interesting note - counter to common thought yet similar to previous research, bullying doesn't seem to be more prevalent at low socioeconomic status. *Rich kids get bullied just as much as poor kids.*

We've gone over that data before. It was a very large sample of kids, which is what's very important for data collection. If you have too small a sample, and most research in martial arts and in bullying have used very small sample sizes, then you can't extrapolate too much from the data you get. When you have small sample sizes, then the data isn't as relevant. It's not as statistically significant. You can do your own research on that if you want to spend a little more time with it, but we got quite a few samples.

Research Question 1: Does Taking Martial Arts Reduce Amount Kids Are Bullied

We already answered this earlier in the look at the data. Let's go into a bit more detail. We can say from the data that the Black Belt students were bullied 64% less than the White Belt students. That's more than any school-based bullying prevention program. This has a few caveats:

- The student gets their Black Belt

- Students that we measured were still training

- The program was similar to the ones we measured (with a good character development program)

Of course, there are (if you want to read my detailed dissertation) many more statistics and details there. Alternate analysis was run against other explanations, like household income, for example, and the best explanation was earning a Black Belt. I would like to remind the reader that when we say bullying in this context this refers to two to three times a month or more! It's not just a little bit of teasing.

Research Question 2: Does Taking Martial Arts Decrease Amount A Child Bullies Others

We did the same analysis of the students regarding whether martial arts would reduce the amount of bullying that the students did. We were open to the possibility that some people worry about – does martial arts increase the amount the kids bully? Is it like some popular TV shows such as *Cobra Kai* where they do martial arts, and it seems the point of learning martial arts is so they can fight the kids from the other school? Admittedly, that's a funny TV show, and it's garnered high TV ratings, but the concern is just how representative is it of martial arts training? In both sides, the "good" karate guys and the so-called "bad" karate guys, both create conflict and seem to revel in bullying. However, this is not the model that we'd like to see in martial arts nor what I'd recognize in any of the hundreds of martial arts schools that I work with or observed. Nevertheless, since this is a common misperception, what does the data show?

Our hypothesis is that children who participate in martial arts for a long time will not bully others as much as kids who are beginners. The main question that was asked in the questionnaire was: *"How often have you taken part of bullying other students in school in the past couple months?"* This is the first and most direct question with bullying that is in the questionnaire that we used. It's a relatively severe question. If they answer positively to this question, it means they've done it two to three times or more in the past months. That's quite a bit. It means they're doing it frequently. They might be doing it ten times a month or ten times a week but at least two to three times a month. A couple points to remember: this is going to be the kids *self-reporting* (so that third grade or up as they have to be able to read and comprehend the question), it's an *anonymous* test, so there's no reason for them to answer anything but honestly.

You might try to make the case that it's possible some of the kids were lying when they took this test. They could certainly lie, and some probably do. But when we compare the data from this questionnaire to the data from other research in bullying, we're using similar questionnaires or the same questionnaires (self-reported kid data) so we're comparing "apples to apples". If they fib about this information, we would expect they will fib about it in the other reported data. If we see bullying reduced from beginners to advanced students, then we're going to expect to see comparative data. If they lied at the beginning, they'd probably lied at the end about whether they bullied or not. We're making the assumption (a reasonable one) that if they do lie and if they do it's going to be factored out in the end.

Anyway, what happened in our data: Nobody bullied anybody. Well, that's a bit of an exaggeration, but it looked like this:

- Beginner students (White Belts): 4% reported bulling other kids

- Intermediate students: 4% reported bulling other kids

- Advanced students (Black Belts): 1% reported bulling other kids

As you can see most of them didn't bully. Beginners bullied about 4% and advanced students bullied about 1%. You might say, well gee, that's a 75% reduction in bullying from beginner to advance and that's a ton! Unfortunately, in statistics, that's not a "ton". The comparison is against the national data which is about 19.3% of kids bully others two to three times a month or more. The problem with our data is that not many kids that *start martial arts* bully other kids (which is arguably good too).

Hardly any kids come into a martial arts school who bully others and say that they wanted to start martial arts. What's the reason for this? Of course, we don't confidently know. One reason could be that if kids are bullying other kids, they wouldn't want the discipline and structure of a martial arts school. If kids are bullying other kids their parents may not feel like they *need* extra self-confidence (which supports some of the other discussions that we've had earlier that kids who bully other kids already have pretty good self-confidence at average or better). They may not be wanting to do martial arts for some of the same reasons that other students might want to start martial arts.

Therefore, we can't definitively say that martial arts reduces the amount kids bully others (we can't say it increases it either though), but the data is still revealing.

There was further analysis done on some of the other questions in the questionnaire that we used – the question above wasn't the only one about bullying others. There were about nine questions that did talk about bullying others in our test we used. Referring to bullying in lots of other ways, included cyberbullying and other different ways that kids bully, and *these did show statistical significance*. Beginners did seem to bully a little bit more than the advanced students. The advanced students hardly bullied at all based on the data from the other questions that we had available. Unfortunately, it wasn't enough to give us what we would call in our academic research statistical significance, but it does indicate that martial arts are very unlikely to increase the amount of bullying. For any concerns that people might have that martial arts would *increase* bullying in kids, that's not what we see. All of these other measurements point the same way – that martial arts reduces the amount kids bully others. We can say that for certain. The amount of bullying decreases. We just don't have many kids that *start martial arts as a bully*, so it's very difficult for us to measure statistically. I think we can say martial arts probably helps and let's keep doing research!

Bonus: What Parents Think!

One thing I'd like to cover is our parent survey. This was an innovative set of questions not to give us statistical data that we can make academic inferences from, but to learn what the parents thought about all these topics.

After their child began doing martial arts, they did notice what we measured in our research. They perceived a 56% reduction in bullying after martial arts, pretty close to what we thought. I mentioned this earlier but it's good to reinforce it. Beginners reported being bullied 27% of the time. This wasn't the parent report, remember, this was the data that the *students reported*. They were bullied 27% of the time, and the parents only thought they were bullied 4% of the time (once they started martial arts). In the general population, kids are bullied about somewhere around 14% of the time. The parents only thought they were bullied 4% of the time. The kids that start martial arts are bullied about twice as much as the average. The parents are not very clued into what's going on in terms of bullying. They don't think their kids are being bullied, they only think they're being bullied 4% of the time. That's a dramatic difference, and it's something important to think about. As parents we should be paying attention to this, but also understand that your kids *probably aren't going to tell you*. Your kids may not even know the questions to ask or the things to say to you and until they do a survey like the questionnaire that we gave out they might not even know what to express.

The questionnaire gives them some framework of what to express. They may say, yeah, that's happening to me, but they may not really know that the bullying is not expected at school because it's so common. This 27% of what they reported compared to the 4% of what the parents' thought was happening is striking.

> **Key Point: Black Belt Parents See Huge Benefits - Appropriately...**

Another item of interest from the parent survey was that after two to three years of doing martial arts, when their kid got to their black belt, 86% of the parents reported improvement, and they felt like their kid would be able to avoid being bullied. For the ability to not bully other kids, 64% reported improvement.

The improvement in parents understanding, 90% of the parents felt like they understood bullying. Which, when we get to training and what to do, most of the time parents don't understand this difference that we've talked about, the difference between imbalance of power, repeated over time, and intention to hurt. Parents don't understand that, just like a lot of teachers don't understand it. 90% of parents got it enough and remembered enough that they understood it. This is a big part of what would help parents and help the kids downstream.

> **Key Point: More Of The Karate Parents Were Bullied As Kids Than Average...**

Also very interesting was that 25% of the parents reported that they were bullied as a kid two to three times a month or more. The same as the question that we asked the kids, and this was 48% more than what our standard data is for the general population. That's striking. So, many of the parents reported being bullied when they were younger, but very few of them reported bullying.

If you take these two things into account, being bullied as a kid and then bullying others, it seems like the parents look very much like their kids.

> **Key Point: Parents Overwhelmingly Reported Better Self Concept (Confidence)...**

98% reported their child improved self-concept which is the reason we expect martial arts helps with bullying! Self-concept is how they felt about themselves. Did they feel like they were good people? Did they feel like they could excel? Did they feel like they could achieve more in their lives? Almost 100% reported improved self-concept. Their safety skills, 99%, which we would expect, and 98% reported that they liked their martial arts experience. This was in all the students, so beginners, intermediate and advanced were all reporting almost the same numbers.

Some of these students might have only started for week, but they felt like they reported improved self-confidence, self-concept, and improved martial arts. Beginners felt this. This is dramatic, and the parent survey, along with the other data, reveals a big picture. Parents were very similar to their kids when they were young, they felt it was important, and they got a lot of other benefits than just the bullying prevention detailed data that we showed. Another question that might be relevant is how afraid kids are of being bullying. One of the things that we talked about earlier is young girls is that they are so afraid of bullying. **They're way more afraid of bullying than they are of death or getting bad grades.**

It was important for us to know how afraid kids are of being bullied by other students, even if they're not getting bullied, and the beginners were much more afraid of being bullied than the advanced. This wasn't as big as the difference in the other data we saw. It wasn't statistically significant, but I want to make sure that we mentioned that we did see a difference.

> **Key Point: Black Belt Kids Tend To Help Others Kids Who Are Being Bullied...**

Finally, the last part is how do the parents feel their kids would react if they saw another child is being bullied. Here we saw what we'd like to see, which is that the beginners didn't do as much. They'd like to help 51% of the time, and the advanced students would help a lot more. It went from 51% to 75% which is a 50% increase. The fear being bullying and the amount that they would help, which we'll talk about later, is a very important element that we want to teach kids.

Help other kids when you see another kid being bullied or tell an adult. That's part of the martial arts process and training that parents likely participate in, and it is taught to kids. To be clear, this is helping, not beating someone up if they are bothering your friend. We did see a very large jump in the data, and because of the numbers, we'd like to do more research on this. That's not considered statistically significant because of the type of survey we used, but it's certainly worth further investigation. As expected, we saw the largest jump in the advanced group in terms of how much they would help other kids. 75% of the advanced group versus 51%, again 50% improvement in that data. Between white belts and black belts, this would be statistically significant.

We can say that from beginner to advanced, you're a lot less afraid of being bullied, and from beginner to advanced, you're a lot more willing to help other kids if they're being bullied. Let's summarize everything that we've talked about.

Conclusion From The Data

Number one, martial arts does have a big effect on bullying reduction. Number two, martial arts does seem to have an effect in reducing kids bullying other kids, and while we just didn't have enough kids who bully other kids and also start martial arts to measure it statistically significantly. It does look like it makes a big difference based on our follow-up analysis. We also saw that black belts fear being bullied a lot less than beginners, and advanced students help other kids a lot more than the beginners.

Helping other kids when they see someone is being bullied also speaks to their confidence, to their ability to be a leader, and to their ability to do a lot of other things in their life and excel on those things.

The next thing I wanted to make sure we summarize here is the parent survey. The parent survey was revealing. First, they do not have an accurate perception of how much their kids are being bullied. They think their kids are being bullied about 4% of the time, but really, it's 27% of the time for beginners. An incredible and potentially dangerous gap. In other words, they think their kids are bullied one third of average but it's twice the average. I do not believe this is lack of care or attention. I'm sure if we surveyed parents in the general population, we would have similar results.

It's also not because they're not watching what's going on. I believe it's that parents are not informed enough about bullying (particularly the truth about bullying that's in this book) and all of its negative consequences. It's a lack of education, and they don't understand the myths that we've talked about here. This inaccurate perception of bullying results in incorrect action and inaction.

The good news for this section of our book is that they do feel that the martial arts programs are helping (and the data shows they're right). They like it, they've rated it overwhelmingly good or great. Even the parents of beginners rated it 98%, 99%, good for self-concept, safety skills, and, of course, for bullying.

There are some limitations in the research that we did. While we would certainly welcome more people into martial arts, the only people that we get are ones that wanted to do martial arts in the first place. We don't know if people that didn't want to do martial arts would have these benefits because, well, they didn't do martial arts. Would this work as well on somebody that didn't have an inclination to participate in something like this? We just don't know, and we can't know, so that's a little bit of a limitation of research of this type. What we do know are the things that we talked about, and that seems very exciting, not just for martial arts but for other types of activities that implement similar types of systems and understand the research that we've presented. It's a tool parents, caregivers, and anyone who wants to prevent bullying can recommend.

Chapter V: Bullying – What To Do?

In this chapter we'll discuss what you can do about bullying if you are a **parent working with your child** or if you're **anyone working with kids**. Much of this also applies to adult bullying as well, and in either case, you'll need to adapt the content to your own situation. Much of this content here is from earlier parts of the book reorganized so you can present in an actionable format.

> **Need Help?:**
> *For specific help on developing a plan in your organization or situation feel free to check out the back of the book to reach out to Dr. Moody who is available for consulting, developing programs specific to your needs.*

Each section represents skills to learn and, while they can be done in any order and addressed separately, the most straightforward way is in the order presented here. As always, the best way to teach a child is to first understand yourself and then work with them. The skills are:

- Recognition
- What Is Bullying?

- Think

- Awareness – When and Where

- Breathe – Four Square

- Decide – What Do I Do?

- Thoughts – Focus Your Mind

- Act

- Body – How Do I Act?

- Distance

- How Do I Look

- How Do I Talk

- Tattling vs Telling

- Lead

- Understand Other Kids

How to Use These Skills

For parents or professionals who work with children, I recommend working with your kids on each skill in order – probably for a few weeks each. It is okay to jump to a specific skill if your situation calls for it. In fact, after you feel each skill is understood, it's a great idea to come back to a specific skill when appropriate. For example, I find teachers referring to the "Tattling vs Telling" skill quite often and I promise you'll find that useful as well!

Let's get started!

Recognition – What is (and Isn't) Bullying?

Bullying is a complicated thing. As we've seen, what people think is "common sense", is almost all wrong about bullying (most things that are "common sense" are wrong, but that's another book). As we mentioned in Chapter 1, the trouble starts with misunderstanding the difference between conflict resolution, bullying, and violence. These are three separate things that need three separate solutions. Remember our Situation Map:

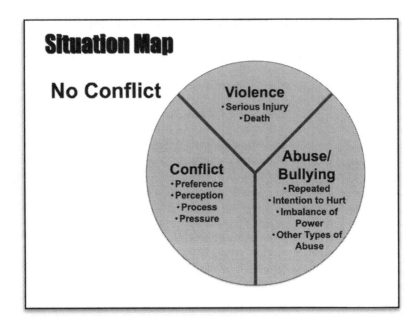

Situation Map

No Conflict

Violence
- Serious Injury
- Death

Conflict
- Preference
- Perception
- Process
- Pressure

Abuse/ Bullying
- Repeated
- Intention to Hurt
- Imbalance of Power
- Other Types of Abuse

To review, if something is violent, you're in danger of serious injury or death. It's not the other two things, bullying nor conflict so the strategies for these situations will never work. You're in trouble, and you need to do some self-defense. This may mean escaping or fighting back. As an eighth-degree black belt, this is a big part of martial arts and it ranges from awareness, violence recognition, escape, violence prevention, and self-defense are among the strategies we need to use. The important point is that if you're in danger of serious injury or death, it's a time to protect yourself - I want to emphasize, **that is not going to work in bullying** or conflict resolution.

Conflict is when two people are having some sort of argument, disagreement, even physically shoving, but it's generally peer-to-peer, or it doesn't meet the definition of bullying. It may not be intended to hurt the other person, they may be just having an issue about a topic (resources, preferences, etc.). Certainly, violence strategies aren't appropriate and neither are bullying prevention ones.

The difference between these situations determines the solutions. Let's discuss further to understand...

Bullying is three things: it's intended to hurt, it's repeated over time, and there's an imbalance of power. With conflict, I might hurt you. I might hurt your feelings. I might make you mad. I could even injure you, because if we're in conflict, and we got in a scuffle. I'm not in danger of serious injury or death. We might have been wrestling over something. I wasn't trying to hurt you. If I was a kid, I wanted that toy. An example as an adult, perhaps we were arguing loudly over a solution for something at work, and we were really mad at each other – maybe we bumped into each other during that argument. As that happened, somebody got scratched, or somebody got a small injury. It's not a serious injury. I wasn't trying to hurt you, but I was too emotional, and things just got out of hand. It's still not bullying. It didn't meet the *intention to hurt* criteria. Maybe I was being a jerk, but I wasn't **intending to hurt**. This is very important. The second thing in bullying is that it's **repeated over time**. This could be something that would be small, it's intended to hurt, and I do it regularly. Maybe something mean every day.

The third thing that's very important in our definition of bullying (and this may be the most important to spend time on) is that there's an **imbalance of power**. In an adult environment, it would be your boss, or somebody that might write a report on you, or it could even be somebody that's bidding on a contract. You're trying to bid on a contract, and the person that's making the decision on the contract could be bullying you. That would be an imbalance of power. Maybe they want some favors, or maybe they're being mean to you, rude, and abusive on the phone. They're using their imbalance of power to get some leverage on you. You may not have the capability to just negotiate. We may not be able to use certain tools that we would have if it's peer-to-peer. We may not be able to be reasonable with the other person, that we have a conflict with. It's not the same. If the intention is to hurt, not just to get resources, or not just to win an argument, or some sort of other thing, then it's an emotional difference.

Bullying has a lot of different components beyond these three pieces. Conflict resolution and violence use different methods for resolution. We must establish, before we deal with bullying, *is it bullying?* I've been in many environments, especially when I teach bullying prevention, where the first thing that happens somebody (because they are focused on bullying because of my talk) calls a situation bullying and it's not.

One time, I was teaching at a school in Tucson, Arizona, when the principal walked in (he should have already been in our training). The principal said, *"Hey, there's a bullying situation. I've got somebody stealing posters off the wall that another kid put up."* Was that bullying? It sounded like one kid was just vandalizing, and the other kid didn't like it. The mischievous kid may not have known the second kid.

I don't know that there was any intention, that there might have been a long-term conflict. It could have been that the first kid and the second kid just had a big fight with each other. We don't know what the situation was. I didn't notice that there was necessarily an imbalance of power, so that would've probably been more of a conflict. They needed to have those kids sit down, or they needed to just deal with the kid that was stealing the posters, who sounded like the problem. There needed to be some consequence for mischievous kid. It may not have even involved poster kid, even though the poster kid got the bad end of the situation, because his posters got taken down. As far as I could tell there wasn't really any relationship between the two boys. There didn't need to be any bullying prevention "tools" used. We need to understand this first if we're going to be good at helping kids. Remember, about a third of kids are involved in bullying, but it's inside of the totality of all conflict. If we don't understand this, we're missing out on a lot of situations.

Think

The next main skill is learning how to **think**: what to think about to prevent bullying from happening and what to do when it does. This requires awareness, breathing, deciding, and focus.

Awareness – When and Where

As a parent or professional - work with your kids on how they think. The first piece of this, when we talk about how they think, is make sure that they know in what kinds of areas does bullying occur. What scenarios? What scenarios might happen, what things are bullying, what things aren't bullying, and that way you can help them with the definition. What's bullying, and what's not. Where do you think bullying would happen? Where do you think bullying would not happen? Where do you think bullying is happening at school? They may, or may not know, and you can help them, but ideally, you'll get them to tell you. Discuss scenarios, come up with lots of examples of bullying.

This can be locations or actions kids take. There are many unusual things kids do – for example we've all heard about swirlies. You all know what that is. Have you ever heard that in some schools, kids get *dirty* swirlies. Imagine what that is... yep, that's when there's poop still in the toilet. Other scenarios where kids are getting pushed, or hit, or yelled at—we've covered a lot of these in our prior descriptions of scenarios, where kids get left out, kids get excluded, kids don't get included in games. What types of different scenarios can happen with cyberbullying?

Another thing to do, is ask what are different spots where bullying might occur? Where are places on the playground where kids get bullied? You can just ask the kids, where do kids bully other kids on the playground? Oh, it's behind the big tree, where there are no teachers. Or it's in the bathroom where there are no cameras. When we do training for teachers, we talk about how they can be distributed around the playground, so they can identify where bullying can happen, and where discipline issues would happen as well. Bullying can also happen in hallways, and mainly where there's not as much adult supervision. You would think that bullying often happens to and from school, but very frequently bullying happens in the classroom with the teacher present.

This is called **preframing scenarios** with kids, so that kids get to think about it, and then when it happens, they won't be as likely to freeze. This isn't intended to make your child scared to go to school and have them worry about all the terrible things that could happen so be mindful of their reaction. That's why it's best if your child comes up with the places and situations themselves and you can be the one who asks about them.

The next part of awareness is how you act. Awareness and focus require keeping their eyes up and paying attention to what's around them. In other environments it's called situational awareness. If you know what bullying is, and you know where it's going to be, then you can focus on it. Scenarios, spots, and focus. This is the first step to being able to prevent bullying. That's the first part of thinking. One of the things with focus is focusing on the kids that do the bullying. You know the kids that are bullying other kids, and who helps them bully. Now, if you're an educator that may be a little awkward in the classroom, because it may be one of your kids who is doing the bullying. You may have to figure out a way to ask that question that's not going to point out other kids, because the kids may not want to talk about it.

Breathe – Four Square

After learning awareness, what happens if something bad (like bullying) happens? First you need to concentrate on *your physical reaction* to the situation. **Breathing** helps you stay calm and keeps you focused.

Breath in, hold your breath, and out. This known as four square breathing, and it comes from the military (and many other sources). They call it tactical breathing or box breathing. In counseling and psychological work, it's four-square breathing. If you breathe in, hold your breath, and breathe out, it does a lot of things for your body. It helps calm you down, it lowers your heart rate, and it helps you make a decision more clearly. Breathe in for four, hold for four, out for four, rest for four. This is helpful for lots of things, such as sports, test taking, and leveling out your emotions.

You can teach four square breathing and use it in many different scenarios. If someone is upsetting them, if someone is pushing them, if someone is doing something they don't like, they can breathe in, hold, and breathe out. You could also prompt breathing, by role-playing bullying situations. Pick a fun code word like "gorilla." Tell them, *"imagine the worst thing somebody would say to you, but don't say it"* (we don't want them to use swear words), and when they imagine that, you can say, *"Well, okay, we're not going to say those words, but imagine somebody saying it when I say 'gorilla'!"*

Now say "gorilla!" and when you do, they imagine it's really one of those bad words, they can practice breathing. They can also – if you're working with a group - pair up, and say, "gorilla." And they've got to breathe and give themselves a message *"I'm ok!"*. They've got to do the four-square breathing. This can be repeated with many other types of actions representing bullying. In a classroom setting, I wouldn't have them push each other, but in other settings, they could. If you're a parent of a child, you could push your kid to simulate if someone pushed them on the playground. In a group, different kids could lead that drill. This is a way of learning to be aware and breathing all at once—learning cognitive, and physical skills together. Next, we'll discuss making decisions under stress.

Decide – What Do I Do?

The next part of thinking is helping kids make a decision *before they are under stress!* Should I walk away, tell a teacher, give myself a message *"I'm ok"*, find a friend? If you discuss and role-play enough scenarios, now they can choose. If they have never built the automatic program in their brain, when a stressful (bullying) situation occurs, they will likely freeze. They won't have a parent, a teacher, or help all the time so they need to learn what to do when they need help. Remember, by definition, bullying includes an *imbalance of power* so advising them to *"fight back"* or *"don't worry about it"* won't likely work.

Sometimes I get asked, "But we can't possibly role-play or discuss all possible different scenarios with kids. There are an unlimited number of variations that can come up." Sure, that's true, however, if you do enough, you're giving the child skills to create new decisions from all of the options they have. If you teach your child to cook enough with you guiding them in the kitchen and showing them techniques, they learn to cook on their own!

So, what's the best decision in most cases? Much of the time it's getting help and support! Getting support balances the imbalance of power. The support could be from their friends or from their teachers. If you're an educator, you've got to have the right situation here. It's easy for you to say, *"Come to me if anybody bothers you,"* but that may be counterproductive for them in some situations. If somebody's getting bullied, and they come to you, as a teacher, that may end up putting them in the crosshairs of the kid or kids who are bullying them. We need figure out a situation where they know that if they do come to you, the process in the school is going to keep the kid and not unintentionally escalating the bullying. A comprehensive school program helps, and again, I do recommend the Olweus Bullying Prevention Program, which has been developed to make sure the procedures in the school are correct and effective. Then, when a kid comes to the teacher, and says, *"Hey, this is happening,"* the process is set up so that kid doesn't get in trouble with the other kids later. We want to make sure that the kids know they can get support by coming to their parents or their teachers. We have to make sure that we know what to do.

Focus Your Mind

One of the greatest gifts you can give your kids (and really, yourself and your friends) is to learn to **focus** your thoughts. This has been repeated throughout the ages in many ways, but here we'll specifically refer to bullying. Thoughts are what causes your child to feel sad, or upset, or anxious, because they're being bullied. It can feel hard to change that, and what we really want them to do is get support or get help, but when they feel this way, it's pretty tough to think rationally.

I want to give you a powerful tool to use here. If your child has continued negative thoughts about themselves, ask your kid what they're thinking when they're feeling emotion. This is pretty hard for a child to verbalize, especially the younger they are, so be patient. When your kid says something like, *"Well, I feel that way because he's right. I'm not good enough."* Resist trying to say, *"Oh, of course you're good enough. I don't know why anybody would say that. Why would you think that?"* This seems a reasonable response for a parent, but to a child this sounds like you're also telling them they're stupid as well, because you are assessing their feelings and thoughts as wrong. It's tough, right? An alternative thing to say might be *"It'd feel bad to me if someone said that to me. I might think that too. Do you really believe that?"* and you can listen to their answer. This shows empathy – *the ability to understand and share the feelings of another.* Be gentle and patient with them in order to help them. Resist telling them how wonderful you see them (I know you do) and why they are wrong about their feelings.

A better way to help is to reassure the child that they can reach out to you. Instead of telling them, *"Hey, that's terrible, I can't believe you think that,"* let them know that you hear and understand how and why they are suffering. If they're getting bullied, and they have negative emotions, oftentimes this negative thought process goes on in their head. It's <u>real</u> for them, and they are *valid emotions*. It does not mean they are correct assessments of the truth. The emotions are valid, because of what's happening in their head.

We need to help them with replacement thoughts and not judge the thoughts that they are having. That's incredibly hard as a parent, because we love our kid, and we think they're perfect and wonderful (and hey! they are!). When they have thoughts that don't feel perfect, it's very difficult to not just tell them, *"Hey, that's not right. You're perfect, and I love you. I want you to know that you're the best thing ever."* Sometimes that gets in, but if they're having these kinds of thoughts, the child may not be able to hear and process those words.

Act

Now we can move on to how to act so we prevent and reduce bullying. If we change our actions, we can keep from being a target in the first place, and if bullying does happen, we can stop it more easily. We'll cover how to manage our body, distance, how we use our eyes and how we talk.

Body – How Do I Act?

In the martial arts we talk about stances all the time. Whether you're in martial arts or not, your stance is important. It's how you present to the world. Your stance is both your attitude and how you physically present with your **body**.

In school when you're taking a class, your stance is usually sitting down. When you're teaching a class, your stance is standing up. What we know is kids that get bullied more are the ones that are going to project (have a stance) an attitude of low self-esteem. Kids who get bullied are going to project an attitude that they're better targets, that they don't have as good a self-esteem, that they are weaker and more susceptible to getting bullied.

What does that look like? It looks like somebody whose glance is downward, who has their shoulders in a weaker position. If we just tell kids to stand up and show us a weak position, they immediately know what that looks like. It looks like shoulders slumped, head down, not looking ahead. We practice this with kids, and we encourage parents to practice this with their children: *"Show me what a weak position is, and now show me what a strong position is."* They're looking upward, their shoulders are up, and they're able to see what's going on, and they look at other people in a confident way.

So much of this is how they present themselves to other people. It's their physical aspects on how they are and their awareness of their surroundings. When they look down, they look weak, but not only that - it's also putting them in a position where they're not aware of what's happening around them because they can't see their surroundings. So, it's not just a weakness of appearance, but a weakness in their ability to do the earlier things we discussed regarding awareness. Essentially this is a poor defensive position.

In addition, most kids have a backpack or something they carry, and typically people carry it in their dominant, usually right, hand. We want them to get used to carrying it in their non-dominant hand so that their dominant hand is free. This is beneficial for a lot of reasons. One is that you can use your dominant hand to do things like open doors or grab stuff, but in a defensive position, now they have their hand available to do things. This is a much better position to be in and much better thing to get used to.

Here's an exercise you do with your kids. Have them walk around in a strong position, backpack on their non dominant side (left side for right-handed kids), hand up, and you say the code word. You could use whatever code word you want, but in our class, we use the code word "bully," and if we say the word "bully," then they'll put their hand up, and they'll keep their backpack shoulder back. Why do we want their backpack shoulder back? Because that way, the backpack can't get grabbed and they can't get pulled around by their backpack, just like a kid with long hair could get grabbed by their long hair. Another byproduct to this is going to be that people will notice you more in a positive way. We know that when you look somebody in the eye, then that is a sign of respect, and you're paying attention to them.

Distance

Another safety item is maintaining distance. If I know I'm in a situation where I'm around a lot of people, and even if I don't know whether they're necessarily dangerous or they might bully me, I want to maintain distance. Maintaining distance means I'm going to be at least two arm lengths away from somebody. In a class, we'll have an instructor with a target that's another arm length, so that they have their arm and the target that's arm length away. The instructor then moves the target around in front of the students, and the students must back up and make sure they understand what that distance is and stay out of that distance. They're not running around, they're not playing, and it's not a game. They need to be able to visualize that distance and know how far away to stay. If you're at home doing it, you would want to pick up something, maybe a yard stick or something that's about your arm length and proceed slowly.

This activity is done so that they can visualize what distance is and learn which distance is going to keep them safe. You move it around, and so the children must move, keeping their eyes up, keeping their eyes on you the entire time. Again, not looking down, not turning their back to you, and not running away or playing. It's eyes on whoever is the designated "bully" at the time and learning exactly how far away they need to stay from somebody - just in case – to be safe. For parents, you can do this by just saying, *"Okay, we're practicing now, so how far away would you need to be?"* If this is a group of people that you don't know, it'd be two arm length away. Now, that's not always possible. Let's be realistic. Sometimes you're in a situation, an event, or a festival, and you're not always able to maintain a certain distance, but this helps you learn to be aware of what distance you are. If you are closer to somebody, then you just need to be paying attention that that's somebody who could grab you.

Understand, we don't want to create an environment of anxiety. We don't want to create an environment that we should fear everybody. What we do want to do is understand that if we are close enough, that we're within two arm lengths distance, somebody could take a step toward us and grab us – so if we are going to have a fun safe time just be aware of the distance to maintain. We need to be sure that we keep our eyes up and pay attention. If we are in a scenario or in an area, let's say on the playground, and if we're a kid that gets bullied, then this would be an important time when we need to maintain distance. If you don't practice this with your kids, they won't understand the spatial distance. Some kids naturally might, but not all of us do, so we need to understand how far away two arm lengths is. That doesn't come naturally to everybody, so it's important to practice it.

How Do I Look?

The next piece that we talk about is facial expression: how we look, how we keep our facial expressions. We've practiced how our body shows a confident look, but we need our face to show a confident look as well. What does that look like? For the most part, if we ask kids that are over the age of about six or seven years old to practice a confident look, they usually know what that means. It looks like their face is staring straight ahead, confident, not looking mean, but confident. When we do this with kids, sometimes they decide that it's a mean look. It's not a mean look. It's a confident look. It just means that I'm looking at you correctly, in your eye. Their eyes are directed straight ahead, and they're also scanning the room to make sure that they know what's going on. Again, we're not trying to create anxiety, and we're not looking for trouble. We don't want to train our kids that you've got to be watching around, looking for threats. That's not what we're talking about. It's just looking around to make sure we know what's going on. This would help them in sports or other things that they do. They're always aware of what's happening in the room around them, aware of what's going on, and start building awareness of what their environments and surroundings are. This is also good training for leadership and the ability to get in front of people, because if you're up there, and you look confident, that translates into any presentation that you might have to give or anything like that. It rolls into more than being safe from bullies, but now I can present myself to other people and later in life, when you have to present yourself to employers or colleagues, you know what a confident look is. If you have the confident look, it builds into your confidence automatically.

This is a good thing to anchor in. When you show confidence, then you feel more confident, even if you didn't feel confident in the first place. A lot of times, kids that are in a new school get bullied. The one thing parents can do is to help them with these things, then they'll start projecting a little more confidence.

How Do I Talk?

Now we're going to talk about voice, which goes along with face. Voice is paying attention to how they talk. In martial arts, we do something called the "kiyap" (in other martial arts it's called something different). That means they yell, *"Yah!"* They yell, and they sound strong, and they practice it. When we do classes with kids, they practice loud yells. They practice a loud one and a weak one so that they know the difference. You inherently know the difference but contrasting the loud with the weak drives the point home. The other thing we practice is saying, *"Leave me alone!"* or *"Just stop!"* in a confident way that communicates they've had enough. they'll stop if you say it in a confident way.

When we're talking about using your voice appropriately, it's important to be serious. That means not to talk like a baby or use "kid" tone – even if they are 3 years old. If you're practicing this for real, and you want your child (or children in your class) to be safe, don't let them get away with baby talk. Don't let them be giggling and laughing when they're doing it because that doesn't project confidence. Not practicing it seriously says, *"Oh, it's a game,"* and they won't translate it as a serious activity. We also don't allow screaming. It's not, *"Leave me alone,"* and they're screaming wildly. It's a *confident voice* that somebody will listen to, not ignore because kids are yelling and screaming all the time.

You want to make sure you look people in the eye (or at their forehead if you're not confident yet or if there's a big imbalance of power). Remember, bullying has an imbalance of power as one of its characteristic features, so if there's an imbalance of power, sometimes it may be very difficult to look somebody in the eye. One trick for that is to look at their forehead. It'll feel easier to maintain your confident tone. Role-play strong and weak tones for all the helping professionals that are working with kids, and role-play different scenarios, talking to teachers about homework, talking to your parents about how you would do different things. What if you made a mistake? How would you talk to me if you broke something in the house? How would you come to me and talk to me about that?

Imagine parents, if you actually role-played and talked to your child about *"how would you come to me if you broke the lamp?"* And you discussed how you would like them to come to you if they made a mistake, so they don't lie about it or hide or hide the lamp or put the pieces of the lamp under the table and hope nobody notices. How would you like your kids to talk to you so that they would know what to do in those situations? What should they do if they made a mistake? Role-playing those situations would allow them then to learn some confidence.

We have three big things here: stance—making sure you control your own physical posture and distance; face—showing a confident look; and voice—how to say, *"Leave me alone," "Stop," "Enough,"* talking in an adult, confident way. If you're three years old, you can learn how to talk in an adult confident way.

Tattling vs Telling

What comes next? What happens after bullying goes on? This is one of the most important pieces. Bullying might have happened, you might have thought the right thoughts, you might have had the right stance, you might have had the right voice. What do you do if you're a kid?

How do you as a caregiver, as a helping professional, as a parent, how do you help a kid learn to know what to do? *We want kids to tell somebody*, but kids get caught up a lot in one big, huge conundrum, and that's tattling versus telling. The problem is that teachers or even parents, have kids telling them all the time, *"Johnny did this, and Sally did that, and Billy did this, and they did that, and they did this,"* and there are kids descending upon them all the time telling them all kinds of things. So, if a kid is getting bullied, and they go to the teacher, sometimes the teacher (understandably) says to them, *"Hey, quit tattling on the other kid."*

Or the teacher may just be so inundated by all these messages from the other kids that they're not going to listen to them. I don't blame the teacher for that, and we shouldn't blame the teachers because teachers have a very difficult job in sorting out what's right and wrong or who is telling the truth or who is just trying to get attention. The solution is to teach kids about the difference between **tattling and telling**, and how to make sure they know how to put the message into a format that the teacher or, frankly, their parents can *hear in the right way*.

If you and your sister have been fighting all day long, and you've been complaining about her, and she's been complaining about you, and you've been complaining about her, and she's been complaining about you, and then something *actually happens* that you need to tell your parents about. Well, it may sound like all the other things you've been complaining about that day, right? They don't really want to listen.

So, what's the difference between tattling and telling? **Tattling** is when you're trying to *get somebody else in trouble or get attention*. If you're a teacher or a parent with a bunch of kids or work with kids all day long like we do, you hear this all the time. They're trying to get somebody else in trouble or get attention for themselves. That's tattling. **Telling** is when you're trying to get *protection for yourself or others*. Telling applies if somebody's getting hurt. That could be hurt in all the different ways that we've talked about in terms of bullying or violence, so you're trying to get protection. Tattling, you're trying to get somebody else in trouble or attention for yourself. If you're a teacher or parent, you need to be really good at identifying the difference between telling and tattling. That's not always easy!

Kids and adults have different jobs regarding "tattling versus telling". As a kid, your job is to decide whether this is tattling or telling *before you go talk to the teacher*. As for us adults – when a kid comes and complains, doesn't it sometimes all sound the same? How can you as a kid know how to say it so it doesn't sound like tattling? How can you as a parent, teacher, or professional help kids know this tell versus tattle thing and maybe more importantly how can you *hear* the difference?

The idea is to show them how to put the message in the right format, and it's important to be specific. For example, "I saw John bullying Sally in the hallway. He knocked her books out of her hands, and he got her friends to laugh and call her names." That would be something that likely a teacher would pay attention to.

You have to decide, as a kid, whether or not you're going to get in trouble with the kid that was bullying, and you have to be strong enough to stand up for yourself and for the other kid if you're going to make sure you tell the teacher. Putting the words in, *"I'd like some help,"* or, *"they need some help,"* makes it sound very different than you just telling about something happening. Adding those words, *what you need*, what you *need for help*, what you *need in some other way*, will make it come across like a telling message instead of a tattling message.

The good news is you're going to have lots of these messages to help with because they're tattling and saying stuff to you all the time. Did you ask me for anything that you need, or were you just telling me about somebody else? Did you ask for something that they need? Do they need protection? No? Then that's tattling. Working through these definitions will help kids get the message. This is a critical part of the skill of learning the difference between tattling and telling – am I getting help for myself or someone? If not it's probably tattling.

Lead

One of the best outcomes we have learned is that kids do want to help other kids. If they are in an environment that they feel safe themselves, the adults around them are supportive and they know what to do, they can turn into kids who help other kids out of bullying situations and be positive leaders in their environment. If you work through all the other skills of recognition, thinking, acting then how to understand other kids will help them and the others around them.

Roles Other Kids Play

What we want to talk about a little bit here are the different roles that kids have in bullying. This a little bit different for adults, so it may be helpful to consider some situations that you might have at work or in other groups as well.

You might have a person that's verbally, or physically bullied, or being cyberbullied, or some other type of bullying towards this kid who's being victimized in some kind of way. Think about this scenario. There are other kids that are involved or other people that would be involved. There are also people who are followers, and they're not starting the bullying, but they're active. They just didn't start it. We recommend the Olweus Bullying Prevention Program. They have something called the bullying prevention circle, which is similar to what we'll talk about today. There are also people who are supporters. They may not actively bully kids, but they're going to be egging people on.

They might be standing on the side, they might be supporting the other kids, they might be telling the followers or the child that started the bullying that they're doing a good job. They might be telling them later, *"Hey, we thought it was really funny what you did to that child."* These kids—the ones who start the bullying, the active kid that didn't start, or supporters—are still involved in continuing this process of bullying.

There are also the passive supporters. They may not start the bullying, but they still like it. They may think it's funny. They may be laughing on the sidelines, and it makes the kid feel worse. Plus, it encourages these other kids in the environment to continue the bullying. Now, there are other kids involved, too, that don't really like the bullying, but they are disengaged onlookers. They may not really care one way or the other.

Then there's also a pretty big percentage, if you look at the data that we talked earlier, of possible defenders. These are kids that don't like the bullying, but they don't know what to do. They think they ought to help, but they don't do it yet. You can imagine this person. They see what's going on, they think it's really lousy what these other kids are doing to the kid who's being bullied, but they don't do anything. They don't do anything at this moment.

Then there's the protector. This is a kid who dislikes the bullying and does something. This is labeled differently in different types of programs, but this protector is what we like our black belts to be in our martial arts classes. We can overtly train kids to do this. For parents, educators, and people that are working with kids, this is a great position that we would like to have kids be in. This might look a few different ways, and we'll talk about how to do this or how to train kids to be in this position. What we like to do, ideally, in any bullying prevention program is move kids this way.

You see a lot of kids that come in at the beginner level and they move on to black belt, you see them be confident enough so they probably could do this. They gain confidence, this innate desire to now go out and protect rather than just stay back or help even the bully. It's not just because they got a black belt, it's because they did all that work, and not just because we teach bullying prevention, because the way that we teach martial arts they just gain that confidence and the important stuff.

If we want to help kids be protectors, we need to tell them specifically what to do. Remember our statistics, about two-thirds of kids are interested in helping. They either would like to do something, but they don't know *what to do* or don't know if the *teachers will be supportive*, or they don't know if the *other kids will be supportive*. There's a larger group of kids and a larger group of people that don't think bullying is a good thing and would like to help.

About two-thirds of kids, from our data, that either don't like the bullying and would like to help or don't know what to do. How can we teach them what to do? Let's talk about what being a protector can be. Now, one piece of being a protector is in the environment that they have in school. What would you think would happen if you're a kid and you're in an environment in school and you're not sure if the teachers would back you up if you were trying to protect the kid, if you thought you'd get in trouble? You would be much more hesitant to act and do something.

One of the problems that kids have is worrying that if they go to protect another kid, what's going to happen? Now, if the kid that protects the kid who's being bullied goes off and punches the kid who's bullying, that's going to be a bad situation already. We don't suggest that they do that. That's not what we mean by protecting. Of course, we would expect that kid to get in trouble. That would be a normal thing that they should get in trouble.

What can the protector do? Well, what the protector can do is a couple things. At the very lowest level, they could talk to the kid after. That way there's no risk for the kid who's being the protector to get involved in the scuffle or get involved in the fight. There's no risk for the kid who wants to be a protector to do something about it to get bullied himself or herself. That's one thing that they could do.

Another thing that they could do is tell a teacher. Now, we talked before about the difference between tattling and telling. Tattling is when you're trying to get attention for yourself or get somebody else in trouble. You have to tell the teacher in a way that you're letting the teacher know, *"Hey, Sally is getting picked on over there and I'm worry that she's getting bullied"* or *"I'm worried that she needs some help."* The teacher would know that this isn't just you tattling on the other kid that's bullying her. If you're a parent or an educator, role-playing through this with a kid would be very helpful so they know what to do.

Another thing that they could do after telling a teacher is talk to the bullied child. Be supportive, let them know they didn't deserve that treatment. The next thing they could do is intervene. The intervention would be, in this kind of case, maybe something very simple like telling the kid who's bullying to stop. What we teach them in our martial arts classes is to put their arm around the kid who's being bullied and say, *"Come on, you don't need that,"* and just take them away.

Now, that's a pretty strong position to be in. You've got to have a lot of self-confidence to be that kind of protector when the other kid is in the middle of getting bullied or getting yelled at or getting pushed or having something more severe happen to them. This level of confidence has to be a lot higher for you to be able to do this.

Ideally, a protector would take action rather than going to a teacher immediately and, depending on the situation, maybe the bullying has already been completed once the teacher actually does anything about it. Of course, they can tell the teacher (not tattle) as well but then they prevent further bullying at the moment when emotions are running high.

It's a little more dangerous for the protecting kid. You have to be careful about whether you're going to do that or whether you're going to be strong enough to do that because you don't want to get in trouble or escalate the situation into a fight. It's important for parents or teachers, or any educators or people working with kids, to not tell the kids to just push the other kid or yell back at them or hit them back.

While you often hear stories of kids (or adults) punching back in some way to solve the bullying problem – and especially to adult men that sounds like a great idea. It's not the reality of bullying. Bullying is an imbalance of power, if somebody's stronger than you or they have better social status, you're not going to get away with that. They have friends. They're usually bigger than you.

Even if you could, you have the ability, the power, the hype, whatever, to take the sort of violent action, it's still not a good idea. One of the first things you learn in martial arts is that you shouldn't be using martial arts on people. You should be using the discipline that you get, the communication that you get. Part of communication and respect is diffusing situations rather than escalating them. Let's say you're going to go protect somebody who's being bullied, imbalance of power, they have friends, you want to diffuse that rather than escalate that. Ideally, everyone gets out unharmed. Then you can go tell a teacher later.

This is why we see such good results in our data when people have done martial arts. We're not trying to tell everybody that they have to do martial arts to learn how to be a protector, but those are some of the skills that we want to transfer to everybody reading about this later. Interventions are not about physically intervening in a self-defense way or to push, or hit, or kick, or anything like that. The interventions are to diffuse the situation, and to remove the kid that's being bullied from the situation. Then, tell a teacher and make sure that they take care of it.

Chapter VI: What To Do If You're A Parent And Your Kid Is Being Bullied

This chapter will focus on the best ways to support your child if they are being bullied. Another great resource in the United States is StopBullying.gov for more information, and I also recommend additional resources like children's mental health professionals and of course your child's school (we'll cover schools in the next chapter).

It Took A Lot For Your Child To Tell You:

Children frequently do not tell their parents that they are being bullied because they are embarrassed, ashamed, frightened of the children who are bullying them, or afraid of being seen as a "tattler." You're probably not surprised after all the data we've looked at but understand that if your child tells you about being bullied, **it has taken a lot of courage to do so**. Your child needs your help to stop the bullying.

Begin With Empathy

Remember we define empathy as the ability to understand and share the feelings of another. Even if you haven't had the same experience as your child, you probably know what it feels like to be in a similar situation. If you can't imagine that... it's time to imagine that. Your child needs first to know that you understand them and how they are feeling.

Be Supportive And Gather Information

It's never good advice to tell your child to ignore the bullying. What the child may hear is that _you_ are going to ignore it. They wouldn't be coming to you if they had the option of ignoring it. Ignoring it may turn in to escalation to a more serious problem. Also remember just because you may feel it's not "that big of a deal" doesn't mean it's not a big deal to your child. Let them know bullying is wrong and not their fault. And you appreciate that they had the courage to tell them about it.

Don't blame the child who is being bullied and at the same time don't assume that your child did something to provoke the bullying. That seems weird, doesn't it? I mean _someone had to be at fault, right?_ Well, first, now isn't the time to establish blame, and it really isn't the point. Here are some things **not** to say:

"What did you do to aggravate the other child?"

"You're just being dramatic!'

"It's not that big of a deal!"

"Well just stay away from that kid and they won't bother

you!"

"Toughen up!"

"Stand up for yourself!"

You could say these things if you want your child to never tell you about problems they have at school again (sorry for the sarcasm). Each of these is blaming the child for the issue. Look, I get it – our parents said this kind of stuff to us, so we figured that was good parenting. It wasn't but don't blame them either – they didn't have this book to read.

So why don't you want to blame the kid who's doing the bullying? At the moment that's not what your child initially needs. They do need you to understand the feelings and the circumstances. You also need to be careful that it's bullying and not conflict (remember our earlier chapters).

Listen carefully and maybe even take notes on what your child tells you about the bullying. Ask him or her to describe who was involved (all parties) and how and where each bullying episode happened. For example:

- Where did it happen?

- When? How often?

- Who was there? Kids? Adults?

- Of course, what happened – but in calm detail where they feel support and empathy?

Helpful Keys

It may seem counter-intuitive but _ask your child what he or she thinks can be done_ to help. Assure him or her that you will think about what needs to be done, and you will let him or her know what you are going to do. **Don't immediately react.**

If you disagree with how your child handled the bullying situation, **don't criticize them**. They're a kid, and they were under stress – how many of us make the best decision "in the moment" and under duress.

Do not encourage physical retaliation _("Just hit them back")_ as a solution. Hitting another student is not likely to end the problem, and it could get your child suspended or expelled or escalate the situation. We've covered this extensively in other parts of this book.

Calm your emotions. It's understandable to be protective of your child and have strong emotions about what happened to them, as well as about how they responded. <u>You have the benefit of time to decide the best course of action.</u>

Contact your child's teacher or principal.

We're going to have an entire chapter on how to talk to educators at your child's school about bullying, however, here is a summary. Understandably, Parents are often reluctant to report bullying to school officials, but bullying may not stop without the help of adults.

Helpful Keys When Talking To The School

Stay calm. **Give the factual information** about your child's experience of being bullied including who, what, when, where, and how that you gathered earlier. If it's written down and the administrator can get a copy, that's better.

Emphasize that you want to work with the staff at school to **find a solution** to stop the bullying, for the sake of your child as well as other students. Your job isn't to suggest how they punish the offending child or how the teacher is supposed to operate their classroom. They're the professionals at the school, and they are going to have to own the solutions.

Under no circumstances should you contact the parents of the student or students who bullied your child. Sometimes this is a parent's first response, but this will likely make matters worse. That's the job of school officials to contact the parents of the child or children who did the bullying.

It's a reasonable expectation for you to **expect the bullying to stop**. Talk regularly with your child and with school staff to see whether the bullying has stopped. If the bullying persists, contact school authorities again.

Summary

You're ready to help kids! Mostly... In real life you may encounter situations that look like bullying but are just conflict between peers. Or you could encounter schools that are not focused on bullying prevention. You might also find a situation we haven't covered here.

I wish there were always straightforward, easy 100% infallible answers for every situation. If I could give you a step-by-step cookbook for everything you could encounter, I would! As we've seen in other parts of this book, bullying is complex, but you have a big advantage now with all of this knowledge and these steps to follow. This will get you through most of what you're going to find.

In the next couple chapters, we'll explore more details on how to talk to school officials as well as helping your kids become more resilient to bullying.

Chapter VII: How To Speak To Your Kids' School If They Are Being Bullied

In this chapter we'll repeat much of the prior chapter but with the focus on the experience you will have when you speak to school officials. This is a stressful position to be in but as we'll see, critical.

Parents are often reluctant to talk to the teacher or principal because they feel like maybe that's not their place. Perhaps they're even worried that if they do talk to the school official, they'll make the situation worse, because the official will inadvertently make their kid stand out, and then it will make them a target for further bullying. These are legitimate concerns. Your child might have even told you, "*I talked to my teacher, and they said something to the class. Then I really got it from the other kids!*"

The problem is that if you don't do something, it will often get worse, so it may not stop unless you **take action**.

The first three key points are: One, understand *it may not stop unless you talk* to the school officials. Two, *keep your emotions in check*. We want to give factual information, and that's why we talked in the prior chapter about make sure you thoroughly listen, provide empathy for your child, and make sure that they're comfortable sharing all the information. <u>Three,</u> and most importantly, ***kids should never have to tolerate bullying*** at school (or anywhere). Yes, in this book we'll relate how it does happen, however that doesn't mean it's ok to happen.

Sometimes the information about bullying is very emotional, and it will likely be hard for your kid to talk about. It'd be hard for them to say what the other child said to them. Maybe it's a bad word that they don't normally say to you as the parent, and if they say that word out loud, they will typically get in trouble at home. Let them know that it's okay for them to say what happened, and it's okay for them to say anything to you as a parent in this situation.

When you're talking to your child ahead of time, make sure that you're fully informed. This is another reason it's important to be fully engaged in what happens, be empathetic, and find out the whole story. Then, when you talk to the school official, you can give factual information (preferably written) about your child's experience and make sure that you tell them the who, what, when, where, and how. The who would include all the kids that are involved, not just the kid who's bullying your child. There are often more kids involved. Make sure that you have a conversation but do it in the right way. (For more information check out the prior chapter)

Let the school know who's been helping, who are the helpers and supporters of your child, and who's been positive, and all the other parties, including the teachers that might have been helpful. The teachers that might have said something and you need to be very specific about it— what actually happened. Try to be as accurate as possible. When did it happen and where, this is very important. Again, bullying happens in all kinds of different spaces. It's very important to know, because maybe there's a hole in where the teachers are monitoring class, and the how (what the bullying was).

Another consideration is that you work _with_ the staff. This doesn't mean do their jobs for them, but you want to help them find a solution to stop the bullying for the sake of the child and be supportive of the staff. Keep in mind that the kids who bully are not doing it because they have low self-esteem or these other myths that we've talked about, and while there needs to be negative consequences for bullying, in the long term, it's not good for any of the kids.

While of course your primary focus is on your child, if you are also focused on the fact that it's not good for the kid who is doing the bullying as well, it will be easier for the school staff to listen to you. It's not good for your child, and it's not good for the sake of the classroom environment and the school. It's not positive for anybody involved. I can't stress this enough. If you communicate with all that in mind, it's going to come across a lot better than if you are just saying, "I don't care about anybody except for my kid, and you guys need to fix it now!" with a bunch of swear words added to it.

The next consideration is do not under any circumstances contact the parent of the student who's bullying. This often is a parent's first response. If you call up Johnny's mom and say, *"Hey, your kid's been bothering my kid,"* it often makes matters worse. School officials have that role, and they need to do their job. When a third party handles it in a less emotional way, the outcome will be better for you. And... what if you find out the information from your child is wrong?

Your expectation should be that the bullying stops. Let me reiterate – your expectation is 100% that this stops. You should not accept that it reduces or only happens once in a while. It ends. It may not be overnight, but you should be talking regularly with your child and with the school staff to ensure the bully has stopped. If it persists, then you should contact the school authorities again.

In summary, for your conversation – when you talk to the school officials, don't hold back with *information* and *questions*. Keep the emotions in-check, understand that this is not good for anybody (even the child who was bullying), and it doesn't help their school environment. Understand also that they may not be aware of the problem. You might feel like, *"You ought to be aware of the problem. You guys are the ones watching these kids. You should be checking the kids in the classroom. How could you guys possibly let this happen?"* That will escalate into a conflict, therefore not helping your child. What's going to help your child is you coming in with the factual information, *"My child's been bullied at school by this child. This is where it's happened. These are the other kids involved. This is when it's happened, and this is what's been going on. Now, I want to work with you to resolve the situation and make sure this doesn't continue."* That's a very common, reasonable explanation. Helpful hint: you will know you're off track if you use the phrase *"you should."*

Written Record

Keep a written record. If your child has told you, or you think that your kid is being bullied, as you're gathering information, keep a written record. In some instances, your child will come straight out and tell you that they've been bullied, here's what's happened, and they'll give you a really good picture of everything. In some cases, you may just notice a mood shift in your kid. There may be something unusual at home, and you may not have a clear indication that something's wrong. It may take you a while before you even make a note of this. Then it gets progressively worse over time. You get some information, and then you get a little more information, and finally you find out hey, my daughter has been bullied for the last six months. This may be very unsettling when you find this out, but it's important to pay close attention to that and then you can write some notes when you first started noticing it when it happened.

If the dates aren't exact, that's okay. The better you can do it, the more helpful it'll be. You want to record the names of the kids involved. All of the kids, not just the kid who's doing the bullying. There're often other kids involved, kids that might be egging them on, kids that might not be the original one who's bullying, but they may be participating later. There also might be kids that are helping your child. Is there anybody helping? Is there anybody your child after the bullying is over? Are they helping and trying to intervene? Those are important ones to write down too, and make sure you make note of them. You want to know when, what, where, and how.

The Meeting

Meet with the teacher and/or the principal and explain everything in a friendly non-confrontational way. Since you get this information, you can explain to them, *"My daughter reported this to me. She said this is what happened, and I know this is not good for anybody in the environment of your school, including the kid who's doing the bullying."* There are a lot of negative consequences for the kids who are bullying as well, so you want to make sure this gets fixed.

Ask the teacher about their observations. They may have observed something. They may have seen some of this stuff. They may have chalked it up to a conflict. They may have not noticed it. They may have thought that your kid was involved as well and was responding back and forth. That's an important time not to get defensive. Maybe your kid was involved with responding. Maybe they were responding to getting bullied, or maybe they were also initiating some of it. Let's wait until we get all the information until we make a decision. We want to know if they've suspected bullying or anything else.

Next, ask how your kid has gotten along with others in class. Have they made friends? Have they been interacting well with other kids? Does it seem like there's a good social environment around them? Have you noticed that they've been isolated or excluded from the playground events or activities with other students? This is important because we want to establish whether or not your child's social environment is good or not. The teacher may or may not have a great understanding of that because they've got a lot of other kids to watch, but you can establish some good baseline information on whether your kid is making friends and playing on the playground? Are they participating in activities? Or are they being excluded from activities? It also will help you get the teacher to pay attention to these things and note them moving forward.

Actions

Ask the teacher what they intend to do about the bullying. Will they be investigating and stopping the bullying? If you're concerned about how your child is coping with the stress, if it seems even slightly severe, ask to talk to the school counselor. This is nice to do for a couple reasons. One of the reasons is that the school counselor can work in conjunction with the teacher to support stopping the bullying in the classroom. Hopefully we're intercepting this when it's more minor. I would much rather you talk to the school when it's not very severe.

Set a Follow Up

Set up a follow-up. Do that the day you meet with the teacher. Don't just say, *"Well, I'll call you."* Set that up at that time, maybe for 30 days later or whatever time period you feel comfortable with. What happens if your kid gets bullied even more severely as a result of this? Maybe for some reason the strategy didn't work, and it made the situation worse. Now, your child might not want to report it to you because the evidence is when he or she reports it, the bullying gets worse. In his or her mind they're thinking, *"I don't want to tell you that it's worse because you're going to tell my teacher, then it's going to make it even worse."* Have the follow-up set so that regardless of what you hear at home, you can then talk to the teacher. If it's better, then the follow-up reinforces the correct behavior that the teacher is doing and everything that's working well. If it's not better, then you can make a new plan.

Expectations

If there's no improvement, you need to speak to the school principal. As a reminder, keep notes. This is not because you're being a lawyer here, but it's so you can make sure you're clear-headed, and you can speak professionally with everybody, so there's less emotion involved. It's very easy for this to escalate into emotion, but then you don't get the outcome that you want.

Your expectation should be that the school staff investigates immediately. If they say, *"Well, we're going to get on that next week,"* as for specific actions and deadlines. Bullying isn't something they get to wait on. They need to do it immediately, and they should inform you of their plan as soon as they do something about it. As I said before, they should let you know what their plan is. There shouldn't be any delay in this. They should let you know very quickly what the deal is. They should be talking to the parents of the child who is doing the bullying. They should be talking to that child and all the other children involved, including the ones who were helping your child, including the ones who were supporting the child who was bullying and any of the involved parents.

Notes on Solutions

It's a bad idea for the school staff to have a joint meeting between your child and the child who bullied them. Remember this *isn't conflict resolution*, this is _bullying_. If the kid who is bullying your child is in a meeting with them, they're already at a higher power level. There's an imbalance of power. Bullying is a form of victimization, not conflict. While you may not be able to talk them out of it - be aware of this.

To expand on this – remember, it's okay to have people "talk it out" if it was a peer-to-peer conflict. It could be an argument or even a fight! However, with bullying, you can't use these tactics. It's more like abuse or victimization.

The school staff should never have mediation or conversation. It will be embarrassing for your child, and it is very likely to make the bullying worse. If their plan is to have your kids sit down together and have them talk it out, you might try to suggest other alternatives if you can. It's fine if you explain bullying, and you can share some of this information with them about how bullying is an imbalance of power. That's not going to resolve the situation. That will embarrass your child and that's not going to make anything better.

What we want to know is what are they going to do so that the kid who's bullying does not do this anymore. That has to do with that child. What are we going to do to support my child who's being bullied? That's the solution we're looking for, not how they're going to mediate. Mediation will not work unless we've got this story completely wrong and there's no imbalance of power and it's a conflict situation. What they should be doing with bullying is meeting with the child who is bullying, and they should be meeting with the bullied child to learn what they've experienced and make sure there's a plan to keep them safe. The school should be talking to them about keeping them safe, how they're going to be supported and feel better if there's any stress or trauma, then to deal with that.

Rules and policies need to be enforced. What are the school's rules and policies? Are they on the website? The school needs to meet with the kid who's suspected of the bullying to make sure they know the rules. Make sure there are consequences and make sure in both cases (all kids and parents involved), the parents know the plan that they know what the plan is and what is tolerated and what is going to be acceptable. What's important here, as well, is there's no blame for the bullied child. Very frequently what happens is they say, *"Well, if you didn't talk that way, or if you didn't wear those clothes, or if you didn't do this or do that, the other kid wouldn't have bullied you."* If we've established that this is a bullying situation, there's no blame involved.

In some cases, you may find the school has insufficient rules or policies. You may not be able to change these. You can still establish and understand the actions that will happen for this situation.

You can still help your child. There may be a lack of social skills or lower self-esteem. Maybe they did wear something that really made them stand out. It doesn't mean we couldn't make some modifications or help them improve social skills or have them talk to the school counselor about how they operate with other kids. But that's not blaming them. That's just other work that we're going to do to help them develop. Long term development in a positive way is a very different thing from blaming them for the situation.

Be patient with the school. Give the school reasonable time to investigate and hear both sides of the story. *Just because your kid said were being bullied doesn't mean that's what happened.* We need to make sure that everything is understood. Of course, there are cases where a kid says they are being bullied, and they're the one doing the bullying. The child said says they are being bullied because they know that school is really harsh on kids who are bullying. and they wanted to get the other kid in big trouble... Educators need to make sure that they're not hasty about making any of these conclusions or jumping to an assessment without understanding the whole situation. The whole process usually wouldn't take longer than about a week. More than a week, it's ok to ask about and it's very important, as with all of this, to do in writing.

Most administrators and staff are very responsive to bullying concerns. We know that they very much want to handle these situations. It doesn't mean some of them don't get through and kids get bullied. If they didn't, we wouldn't have 19% of kids bullying other kids and 14% of kids getting bullied. So just be persistent, make sure that you keep good notes and follow these rules and you'll get good results most of the time. Sometimes you don't get good results, and then you must make some other decisions.

Written records, again, are very important—yours and ask the school to keep a written record. I get asked a lot about if and when law enforcement should be involved. Law enforcement gets involved when there's serious physical injury or assault. If a kid's getting pushed that probably isn't physical injury, but if a problem persists or escalates, and school officials are unable to stop bullying, some parents have consulted attorneys. That's one reason that written records are emphasized. It's also very important that, if law enforcement does get involved, you have a written record and have as much information as possible. Make sure that you understand all these situations before you would escalate into more serious steps, however, as soon as there's serious physical injury or any kind of injury, then we want to make sure that we take the appropriate action.

Summary

Bullying happens in every school. If it does happen to your child, this chapter can help prepare you. Also, if you take action when your child is being bullied, chances are that there are other children in the school who are having similar experiences. You're helping them!

One thing that's very helpful is if your school has a bullying prevention program like the Olweus Bullying Prevention Program or another evidence-based program (see the earlier chapters). This is a great start to reduce bullying and improve the entire school environment including grades! If your school does not have official anti-bullying policies or an active bullying prevention program, work with other parents and your school officials to develop one.

Chapter VIII: Bullying Resilience

Let's discuss how can you help your kid be more resilient to bullying. The reality of it is that sometimes there will be bullying in school, and we want to help develop kids that are strong, confident, and aren't going to be bullied as much.

We've talked about our study of martial arts and how that is an activity that helps. But one of the activities, in addition to martial arts, is encouraging your child to build other skills, encourage their talents and positive attributes. This helps your kid's self-esteem. Building your kid's self-esteem will help them be more resilient. If you remember, we talked about kids who get bullied tend to have lower self-esteem. Some of the way you can overcome that is start building self-esteem. Activities like athletics, music, art, and additional help in school if they need it can help them feel confident about what they're doing among their peers.

We reported in Chapter 4 that martial arts is a special case of this (we consider it a development activity rather than a sport), so it serves as an example since it's specifically a high self-esteem builder. What we know from martial arts is that when kids get their black belt (that takes about two to three years), they're less likely to get bullied compared to any school-based bullying prevention program that we've ever measured. That's an exciting result. We know that other activities they do, if they're involved in other things, does reduce the potential for them getting bullied.

Another thing to do is encourage more contact with friendly, positive peers. It's important that they're peers, kids their own age and with similar interest levels. It could be in or out of their classroom. They have other friends that they can spend time with, and they learn to do more collaboration and learn to do more work. This helps them gather a larger social group and helps them build more confidence, as well in their own social skills. It can make them feel like they have outlets other than school, where the primary instances of bullying happen. They can have some relief time.

A special note with gifted kids – often they will get along with kids older than them who have similar interests and intellectual capacities better than kids their own age.

There's no research to suggest that this should be discouraged.

Next would be safety strategies. Safety strategies can help them understand when it's okay to ask for help from an adult, when they're feeling threatened, what bullying is like, who he or she should go to for help and role-play that:

"If somebody pushed you, what would you do? Would you push them back? Well, if you do, you could get into trouble, and if they're bigger than you, then that's probably not going to work out too well. So, what would you do then? Could you get away and get some space? And then what would you do? Would you go and get some help?" "Yeah, that's a good idea." "Who would you get some help from?" These are reasonable things to talk to them about this. Role-play through those and have fun with it. Make sure your child knows that telling and reporting bullying is not tattling.

Telling or reporting is trying to get help, and this doesn't have to be a bullying situation. This could just be, *"Hey, Mrs. Jones, I would like some help on my homework, or I would like some help on this problem."* That's not tattling. That's just asking for help. That's telling.

We should also note that it's important to determine if there a problem with learning or social skills. Does your child need a little bit more training on certain social skills? Or do they have a hyperactivity or impulsivity issue? Are they talking a lot or are they doing something that's triggering some bullying? This doesn't mean it's okay to bully them. If your child has an ADHD issue or there's something, maybe they have autism, something else going on. Those kids tend to be bullied more. It's never okay to bully, however what it may mean is that you can help support them by helping them with social skills, with some other things that they can learn, to help them make more friends, to help them do other things. The other kids may be reacting to what they're doing because maybe they're standing out, or they're easy targets or they may be annoyed by them because they're doing something in class that might trigger the other child. You can help your child learn some different ways of adapting so that it helps them in general work with all other kids, not to placate a bully or anything like that.

Who's good to work with your kids on that? Counselors are great. I, as a counselor and psychotherapist, recommend counseling for kids. It's a very underused strategy, instead of a commonly used tool for development and support, thought of as a last-ditch effort when people have major issues. In addition, there are a lot of classes and programs for kids. I think all kids can benefit from them, and I encourage you to seek those out.

All of what we've discussed are wonderful to role-play at home, even the social skills and the other interactions and listening that we've talked about in this book. It's important at home that they have a good environment so that they can talk, and you can listen and show empathy when they have challenges. Also, an environment where it doesn't mean they get away with anything they want, or they are overly coddled or you're overly permissive, but rather an environment where they have a strong support structure, and they get pushed hard enough to accomplish goals so that they build strength, talents, and skills.

The balance of those things is very important at home. Those are important to maintain so that kids are resilient to bullying. They're not going to be resilient to bullying if they aren't constantly nudged and pushed by their parents to accomplish things on their own. Then, when they go out in the world and somebody throws them a curve ball, like what a bully does, they're going to be able to handle it. At the same time, they need to be able to know that when they come and talk to their parents about something really challenging, that it's okay, and their parents are going to listen. Those two things need to go hand in hand. That's not always easy for us as parents. This is a challenge that we need to accept as parents as we work with our kids.

There are some things we can do: help kids develop talents, encourage kids to make contact with other kids in his or her class, make sure that they're in a supportive environment, help kids meet new friends outside of class, and teach kids safety strategies. If this part of the playground is always where kids get bullied or get picked on, that may not be the best place to go. Make sure we role-play when reporting should happen, when role-play isn't happening, know the difference between tattling and telling, find out if there's any social skill issues that we can help our kids with. We all could use some help on improving social skills and how we interact with other people at any age. Make sure that home is an environment that pushes them hard enough and makes sure that it's supportive enough, that they can talk to you about anything. Those are some of the skills that you can use to help make sure that you understand how to work with the school administration and also make your kids resilient to bullying.

Chapter IX: Adults Bullying Adults

When you're over 18, you've graduated high school, and maybe you're going to college where there can be bullying between teachers and students. How would bullying happen there, and what is the difference between bullying and teachers that are just not good teachers?

Adult bullying can happen in lots of different ways and lots of different situations. My mother was a nurse, and she would tell stories about the doctors. She was born in the 1920s and was a nurse in the 1940s, so can you imagine the types of scenarios in that day and age? Doctors were considerably more high status than they are now. There was a big difference in power, and doctors just ordered nurses around whenever they wanted. Both gender difference and status difference applied. There are a lot of situations with adults where the complexity of the power dynamics can be huge.

There are a few different levels here. When you have a teacher, especially a professor, there's an age difference. A lot of professors are older, have authority because they're the teacher, and they have godlike powers to decide who passes and who doesn't pass. This is a built-in requirement of bullying, an imbalance of power.

The professor could humiliate a student. If I'm a teacher, and you ask me a question, it could be legitimate or it could be kind of a dumb question, and a teacher could say, *"We just went over that. Were you not listening? Were you not writing anything down?"* This could be legitimate, even from the teacher's point of view. The teacher could be frustrated and not necessarily trying to attack this student. Maybe they did cover it. What may come across is the teacher is humiliating the student in front of their peers. This could be just a bad teacher, or it could be a teacher that is *intending* to harm.

Perhaps they get their own reinforcement (i.e. they like it – feeling the power). Perhaps they like making the students feel bad. Or managers, when we're talking adult in the workplace, a manager might like the power. They might like to make their employees feel bad because it makes them feel good. I see this with people that aren't very well developed. Sometimes with people with personality disorders or some other issues might want to make another feel lesser, and that's an intention to hurt.

The third component to bulling is that it's repeated over time. This could be a teacher who repeatedly grades hard on your papers unjustly, repeatedly refuses to see you in office hours, refuses to give you good advice, or repeatedly humiliates you in front of the entire class. Not all of it is with the intention to hurt sometimes, but some of it is.

This can be true of a type of manager in a work environment. The manager could be bullying everybody. It could be repeatedly embarrassing, humiliating, or sending messages. There are bad managers and bad educators who treat everyone poorly. If their intention is to hurt, it's different. For some, their skillset is so limited that they always sound like they're embarrassing somebody, and perhaps that's how their professors talked to them, that's how their managers talked to them, or maybe they've got problems in their own life. They've got horrible life at home. They're getting divorced. Their whole family is doing terribly, and they don't have any money. They could have all kinds of other problems, so when people ask questions, and they're in a bad mood, they snap back at them. That doesn't immediately mean it's bullying.

It's a different problem if a manager is doing a bad job, or a manager is having a bad day, a professor's doing a bad job, a professor's having a bad day. Professors don't always get as much training on how to be a teacher and how to educate people as they could. We know that because part of their job is research. The same is true with managers. Managers don't always get the support they need to be managers.

Bullying puts the person getting bullied into a conundrum, because now how do I fix this when it's my boss? How do I fix this when it's my professor? When we were talking about kids *you had somebody to go to*, which was your teacher or your parent. *You had a **support authority***. But, as an adult you don't necessarily have an *alternate **support authority*** if it's your boss or your professor, who do you go to?

I'll give you a few scenarios. Let's say you're working for a small company, and the person you're working for owns the company. Who are you going to complain to about the bullying? You could complain to the human resources director, but the person that owns the company is the one that's bullying you. Even if it's a more hierarchical company where the manager has a manager, if you go to the boss of your boss, and they don't handle it well, you're at risk, and now your boss is going to be upset with you from then on. If you go to your boss's boss and the boss's boss comes down and yells at your boss because they're not necessarily handling it well, oh boy—now work is going to be unpleasant.

What can help is understanding the difference between bullying and miscommunication or bad management. Is it bad management, bad teaching, miscommunication, or is it bullying? Is it bad communication? Is it a miscommunication? Is it bad skillset? Maybe the manager just has a bad skillset. That's not your job as an employee to fix, but at least you can identify that and then work around it. If my manager has a bad skillset, get a different job if you need to, but you can then understand that and work around it. It's not bullying.

If it's a miscommunication, that's something you could work with. Is it bullying? Then we know maybe I have to do something else. That's the first part of resolving the situation. Which of these boxes does it fit in, and then I can try to figure out what to do.

In one of these built-in imbalance of power situations, you may also be realizing you're stuck there. You can't just walk away from the situation. You may need the income. It may be your dream job (except for the boss). It could be the only professor who teaches a class that you need to graduate. You're stuck, and unfortunately, this happens a lot.

That's why it's important to know what you're dealing with. Is it that they have bad skills, or is it a miscommunication, or is it bullying? If it's bullying, at least then you can try to figure out what the next step is. Now, what would I do if I go talk to the boss? When we were talking about kids, we talked about the difference between tattling and telling. Believe it or not, this applies here too. If you go to your boss and say, *"Hey, I've got a whole bunch of bones to pick with my direct boss,"* or the boss's boss. If you go to your boss's boss, or you go the dean of the college and make a big scathing report about your professor, that's going to get your professor in trouble. That's going to get your boss in trouble. They're not going to be very happy with you. You have to be very careful about how you approach this, and the tattling versus telling identification is important. Am I trying to get help for myself, or am I trying to get somebody in trouble?

When I talk to adults, much of the time when I hear them complain about other people, they *want to get the other person in trouble*. It could be that it's serious or not, but when they're mad, they want to tell me why the other person is a jerk. They don't want to just try to get help for themselves. Truthfully, if it's bad skills or a miscommunication, have at it. You can probably tell somebody that they're a jerk or that they're not very good. But when it's bullying, they were intending to hurt you. If you have identified that they were trying to hurt you, you have to go to the person you're trying to get help from, and you have to try to get the help. Your main objective is not to ask to get them fired. Your main objective isn't to get them in trouble. Your objective is: *"I'm having trouble working right now because of these reasons. I would like to have some help in my current work environment."*

It's an "I" statement. *I'm* having trouble. Then at least you'll have more of an opportunity because you weren't going in trying to get them in trouble. It still may work that way because what you can't control is that the boss's boss isn't also a bad manager and beats this guy up and goes and yells at him. It's unfortunately something you can't control. You can do the best job you can. Same with the dean. You don't know that he's not going to come down and bully this guy, bully the professor, and get him in big trouble. It's a delicate situation. The best thing to understand is that complicated situations, which is this, are going to have complicated solutions. Don't expect simple solutions for complicated problems.

Adult Bullying

The first thing to do in any of these situations – determine whether it is conflict, violence, or bullying. Is it the three bullying criteria? Intention to hurt, imbalance of power (this will be obvious if it's a manager-employee relationship), and is it repeated. Or is it one of these other things? Is it bad communication or management skills, a miscommunication or misunderstanding. Maybe it's a high-pressure situation and everyone is under the gun. If it's one of the other things, handle it differently. If it's bullying, then make sure you "tell not tattle" like we told the kids. I know that sounds a little sophomoric because we're talking about adults, but make sure you're just communicating to try to *get support and help for yourself.*

Here's an example: Let's say you're working for a small business, and your boss is also the owner. It's just the two of you. Evaluate: is it communication, is it bad skills? Lot of times it's bad skills. This person doesn't know how to be the world's best communicator because they're worried about making lawn furniture or whatever the company makes. So, understand what it *is* before what to *do*. The rules still apply. When you go to them, you ask for help and support, not complain about their behavior. I'll repeat: *help* and *support*. It sounds like this: *"I'm having trouble doing my job, and I'm struggling at work because of this. I need some help with this."* It changes the communication pattern with the boss versus, *"I can't stand it anymore that every time I come to work you complain that I'm late but I'm not late. You said that I was late by two seconds."* The best shot you have is ask for help and support and use specific language. If you change the communication pattern you use with people you can hopefully have your best shot at keeping them from bullying. Now, if they're really, truly *intending to hurt you,* intending to cause problems, you'll need to use a different strategy because talking it out won't work. Of course, another option is to not work there anymore, but as I mentioned, that may not be possible. It's not always as easy as just quit the job if the boss is giving you a hard time.

The levels of consequences can be different for kids, and nowadays there's some argument that kids can't get the level of consequence that they used to be able to. It's changed over time, but with kids, in theory, there's a shell that's governing them called parents, teachers, or some authority (for example a church official). Whereas with adults, it's kind of a free for all, and built in is almost always this imbalance of power. Even consider if you're a consultant, an independent contractor, or you're self-employed. You don't report to anybody right? You're your own employee. Well, guess what? You've got people that you contract with, that you consult with, and they could absolutely bully you because if you don't get the work done in time, even though they want stuff that wasn't in the contract, *and* they're being completely unreasonable. What are you going to do? You want their business. And they could abuse you.

Conflict resolution will work if it's bad communication. Conflict resolution will work if it's bad skills. Conflict resolution strategies won't work if it's bullying because now the other person *doesn't need to resolve the conflict _fairly_* since they have an imbalanced power. I'm your boss. I don't need to resolve conflict amicably. Just do what I say. So, conflict resolution won't work then, and though what you'd like to do is get some third party or power to help, but in some cases no third party exists. You're on your own. In that case, you do the best you can to try to get the bullying to stop, and you've got to work with that person yourself, so it's a more challenging situation. Imagine you're a kid in school. Somebody's bullying you, and you've got to only deal with that kid. It's a very difficult situation.

Chapter X: Conclusion

In this book we've covered a lot of ground, but I know it's never enough. Research in the field is ongoing, and I always encourage you to add to your knowledge of current information not just on data but on different ways people (both kids and adults) bully others. Stay refreshed on how to watch out for bullying, how to prevent it, and how to resolve it so it makes the environment better.

Make no mistake kids are getting bullied as you read this book. In a school, on a playground, in a church, at the market on the internet, over their phones—they are getting bullied in every place you can imagine. Adults are getting bullied as well in all the places and spaces that you are. If it was obvious, we'd have an easier time identifying it. It looks and sounds like everyday conversation and "fun" talk, but it's truthfully abuse.

This abuse has far-reaching effects in the short and long term on both the bullied, the one who's doing the bullying, and everyone around them. It ranges from anxiety to poor grades, to physical ailments, to depression, to felonies, and even suicide. That means we can't wait till these things happen to take action. It's all of our responsibility now that we have the information and knowledge to stop ignoring the truths, stop believing myths that are at best negligent and at worst harmful, and start doing!

Thanks for your commitment to reducing bullying,

Greg Moody, Ph. D.
Master Instructor

If You Would Like To Work With Dr. Greg Moody, Master Instructor

There are a variety of ways to work with Dr. Moody on a limited basis.

For speaking (including keynote speaking and training) and seminars. To schedule with him, email Greg@DrGregMoody.com and provide:

- Full contact information for all representatives

- Topic (in detail)

- Your organization's complete information and structure

For consulting. To schedule with him, email Greg@DrGregMoody.com and provide:

- Full contact information for all representatives

- Scope of work, including key goals and metrics

- Your organization's complete information and structure

More Stories From Dr. Moody's Events, Seminars and Work:

Great information to help breakdown conflicts and resolution outcomes! I thought I was attending to help manage my staff but took away very useful tools for my marriage and family relationships as well! Thanks!
Dr. Emily Hurley, Conway, AR

The conflict resolution seminar with Dr. Greg Moody helped me to see where to focus my efforts when conflicts arise with clients. Learning how to narrow in and build empathy with the client is a game changer that will reduce heated conflicts going forward. –
Joshua Booth, Lehi, UT

*Dr. Greg Moody's lecture on conflict resolution with both informative and practical I'm certain it will be able to use this and both professional and personal lives. I highly recommend that anyone who is interested in improving their relationships in business as well as personal relationships participate in his lecture. – **Gerald Dunn, Poughkeepsie, NY***

*Dr. Greg Moody's presentation on Conflict Resolution was clear and straightforward. With his descriptions of the traps we fall into, it was easy to recognize how I deal with conflict. The steps for having good conflict will change the way I react to disagreements and lead to getting decisive results instead of unresolved matters. I now have new tools to use to solve issues both at work and at home. I know this will result in more positive relationships with my family and co-workers. This seminar will help anyone who has arguments that don't settle the issue. – **Laura Sanborn, Chandler, AZ***

*I would like to express my appreciation for your informative presentation on conflict resolution. I really learned a lot and I believe that this will be a valuable solution to a number of different situations including workplace, relationships, family, and businesses. I even gained some insight about my own issues with conflict resolution- so on a personal level it was very valuable as well. – **Diane Reeve Kirby, Plano, TX***

I attended Dr. Moody's Conflict Resolution Program today. It was extremely informative and made me aware of some of the ways in which I contribute to negative conflict. I hope to take a refresher course and delve into some of the topics more. **Debbie Kalgren, Plano, TX**

Thank you for the excellent presentation on Conflict Resolution. It was very detailed and informative. Now I will have better tools available when the need arises. - **Dwayne L. Flees, Grand Rapids, MI**

The "Introduction to Goal Setting Workshop" led by Greg Moody covered the basics of goal setting and the difference in success rates when using goal setting to plan your future. The workshop was interactive and had everyone delving into their future dreams and plans to create a tangible list of goals. Fourteen people attended from our department and they all were very interested in the workshop and the benefits of goal setting. Greg kept everyone focused and moved quickly through the process. Our employees enjoyed the workshop, found ways to relate it to their personal and

*professional lives. They would like to attend additional
workshops with Greg to continue their development.
For many this was their first exposure to goal setting. -*
Julia Villanueva, Banner Health, Phoenix, AZ

*I just had to tell you what an informative and
enlightening presentation on Attachment theory you
gave. It was clear and concise and explained a lot of
things I have encountered with both kids and adults.
The only thing that I would add is that another
presentation would be most appreciated! Thanks so
much for inviting me to attend. -* **Diane Reeve Kirby,
Plano TX**

*Dr. Moody helped us change our program from top to
bottom: curriculum, memberships, programs, pricing.
the result: our business has doubled! don't miss this
seminar! –* **William Babin**

*We were watching your seminar today at Olson's, and I
just wanted to say thank you! I went into my evening
class with greater confidence and a clear action plan to*

*manage behavior. Totally in tune with what Master Olson teaches us, and the graphic with the target was really helpful. Thanks so much! – **Bekah Price, Johnson City, TN***

*Thank you, Ch. Master Moody, for a fantastic virtual seminar this past Saturday. An awesome event that challenged our students and ourselves. Amazing opportunity to learn an incredible amount and our best renewal day ever!! – **Chuck Vertolli, Yi's Vineland, Vineland New Jersey***

*Master Moody is a great speaker. He inspires me each time I go to one of the seminars that he speaks at. - **Melissa Bosstick, Owner, Bloomington ATA Martial Arts Owner***

Having taken several seminars that Master Moody has taught I know first hand that he is an excellent speaker & teacher. I highly value the curriculum he has developed and his vision to implement it into the everyday classroom. He has also been instrumental in helping the American Taekwondo Association achieve the next level in presenting a cohesive and professional image. - **Nick Keene, Owner at Keene's ATA Martial Arts**

Master Greg Moody is an awesome highly skilled martial art instructor, educator, and businessman. His knowledge and skill is a key element to our organization continued success. - **Eddie Murphy, Owner/Murphy's ATA Martial Arts Academy at Murphy's ATA Martial Arts Academy**

Greg is passionate about what he does! Nothing bears repeating more than that. He motivates those he works with to feel passionate too. Greg pulls no punches and tells you like it is, which really is important when you're hiring someone to help you with your business. - **Keith Shoup, Experienced Instructor growing leaders and developing people physically and mentally**

Master Moody is an excellent instructor and communicator. He obviously cares very deeply about changing people's lives in a positive manner. Master Moody is an excellent instructor and communicator. He obviously cares very deeply about changing people's lives in a positive manner. - **Melynda Cordry - Martial Arts Instructor, Owner/Chief Instructor, Bullying Prevention Specialist, Taekwondo and Weapons Instructor, Self Defense Instructor**

I have had the pleasure of working with Greg on a few occasions. His work ethic is beyond reproach. He is reliable and always follows through on his commitments. He has a standard for excellence and goes the extra mile to complete commitments on time. This has earned him the respect of friends and business associates alike. His dedication and skill as a businessman has caused his company to grow and compete in his industry. He has years of training in martial arts, with a special emphasis in working with children and families. I proudly recommend Master Moody for any business endeavor that he wishes to pursue. I am confident that his efforts will prove *beneficial to anyone that chooses to do business with him as well. - **Jimmy Mack, CEO at Master Mack Marketing***

*I have trained under Master Moody for many years learning TaeKwonDo. He is a motivational instructor and always takes the time to go the extra mile to make sure that I am progressing as a martial artist, instructor and leader. He has earned my respect as a black belt, a Master Instructor and as a person. - **Dr. William Sanborn, Jr, Engineering Fellow at Raytheon Missiles & Defense***

*Dr. Moody is one of the most focused and passionate people I've ever had the opportunity to work with. We worked together on an ambitious project that required extensive research and planning, and the ability to aggregate the large volume of input and present it in a substantive manner to the project team and company licensees. Dr. Moody took the lead in moving the project from a concept into a fully developed and well executed endeavor, and it reaped dividends for all involved stakeholders. - **Ian Truitner, RANDIAN***

Greg Moody, a Master Instructor for the American Taekwondo Association (ATA) epitomizes the professional martial arts instructor and business owner. His concern for our nation's children is evident in his tireless work with anti-bullying programs for which he is a subject matter expert in the ATA, training thousands of other instructors in the Olweus Bully Prevention system. - **Anthony Hubble, Enterprise Service Manager at ALAKA'INA FOUNDATION**

I have known Master Greg Moody at least 5 years as owner of the KarateBuilt studio that my wife and children attended. Master Moody has shown his passion for teaching Taekwondo. He is a great instructor and gives his students quality training. I have witnessed Master Moody going out of his way many times to make sure that a student gets whatever training is needed for them to excel. - **Bob Frace, Freelance Video Editor / Videographer**

I have known Master Moody for over a decade. Master Moody has given several seminars on how to run a successful martial arts school and how to help it grow *and retain students and instructors. Each time I have had an inquiry regarding this topic, Master Moody has always provided me with sound advice.* - **Lisa Marie Tuzon, Program Director and Certified Instructor**

Great seminar Lots of useful information – **Gene Paltrineri**

Webinar was very informative and directly to the point. Discipline is lacking in most schools. This totally reinforces our thought process and motivates us to stay on course. – **Jason Johnson**

Chief Master Moody again hit it out of the park with his webinar on Classroom Management. Thank you, Chief Master Greg Moody. – **Marty Callihan, Santa Rosa, CA**

I liked the reference material recommended (which I have ordered!). Clear cut instructions and explanations for WHY it works. Already started implementing (we *did have a lot of good ATA structure in place) and seeing great results! – **Jerry Vonphul***

I have watched the video to the end, it really have a good stuff, discipline is something I am struggling with and ideas I got from the video I will try and implement them, target behavior and 1,2,3 time out, I like that one. Thank you Master Moody for sharing with us it helps us to do things better in our schools. –
Keorapetse Mogopodi

*Ch. Master Moody's great insights and practical application have our classes and our school operating at a higher level than I could have imagined. Thank you sir! – **Chuck Vertolli***

*Very good webinar. I always tend to agree with most things presented. And agree to the discipline and using "Sir" or "Ma'am" – **Brett Hanson***

I like the suggestions presented as for the most part they reinforce what I do and give me a few other ideas to work into my classes. I have posted it to my school page so that my instructors can see it too. — **Ronda Bourdage**

Great — **Yahya Sigidi**

I liked the simplicity of the discipline and what aspects of discipline I am using right now that I can beef up to make the classes better! — **Theresa Vonphul**

Master Moody's webinar was very informative. His PowerPoint presentation made it incredible easy to follow along and learn from him. He knows his stuff. I highly recommend joining his next webinar. — **David Hirst**

Another valuable webinar by Ch. Master Moody! The way the information was presented it was easy to understand and better yet simple to implement! Looking forward to the next presentation!! — **Steven Seme, Rosemont, MN**

*This was full of good information. No games. Formal curriculum that references the youth and adult curriculum. Follow up cards and contacts. Much useful info. – **Dennis Fivecoat***

*Awesome!!! Master Moody never fails to deliver the best content (Value from start to finish) What I love about his seminars is the fact that he and all of the presenters are true martial artists with multiple successful schools, most Martial arts consultants these days don't even have a school...LOL.....If you are looking for the real deal you have found them. - **Paul Mormando, Brooklyn New York***

*I'm enjoying the information that has been coming out of these presentations hosted by Master Moody and his panel. There is always something that I can take away to implement into my own school. I continue to look forward to future webinars. – **Peter Wetherspoon***

I haven't attended a seminar or webinar in a while i listened to the preschoolers one. Totally outstanding and mind numbing with motivation. I just personally what to send a blackbelt Shoutout to you and the rest of the people involved. Great job. My mental curriculum has been rotated. I would love to have the class report card 6 life skills and class planner and anything that you have available. This webinar is on a 5 star master level. If it means anything to you this is what I so desperately needed. Thanks a PILE. – *Jerry Kidd*

Chief Master your seminar on Attachment and how it can affect how people interact with one another was insightful. Having this information available may allow us to give others a little more "grace" when behaviors come out that are unexpected. Knowing where these could come from will help us in our interactions with our clients. I am looking forward to your next seminar! - *Dwayne L. Flees, KarateBuilt Martial Arts Grand Rapids, MI*

Always good, usable information for us to run an even better karate program. Thank you for your hard work putting these webinars on. – *Megan Blanchard*

Absolutely outstanding information how to conduct preschool students from 3 to 5 years old I Always have challenges working with these small young member students So yes a give to this webinar seminar five starts thank you! - **Paul Talamantez Sr. – San Antonio, TX**

Here's What Teachers Have Said About Instructors Dr. Greg Moody, Has Trained:

"The instructor was able to garner the attention and discipline of multiple students who struggle everyday. He taught safety information which these days is crucial for children to know. I highly recommend this opportunity!" **Mrs. Legro, Desert Willow Elementary School**

"As a teacher I appreciate the self-control & respect aspect and the kids absolutely loved the class! We used the classroom calendar to countdown to our next class ☺*"* **Ms. Courtney, Goddard School**

*"The lessons taught during the demonstration were useful. The kids had fun but they had to listen at the same time." "This is a great program that the kids have a lot of fun with while learning." – **Miss Wilson, Stepping Stones Academy***

"Strategies were appropriate and fun for students!" – **Ms. Katy Jordan, Desert Trails Elementary**

"Schedule It! Very fun for the kids and teaches them to be respectful and disciplined" – **Ms. Garrett, Stepping Stones Academy**

"Fantastic Experience!" – Ms. Yannitelli, Wildfire Elementary

"Students are attentive and willing to focus on skills like respect / discipline." – **Ms. April Elmore, Cerritos Elementary**

"I would definitely recommend this to all teachers at any grade level. The kids love it and it's great for them." – **Ms. Hoffman, Colina Elementary**

"We noticed a change in manners and respect almost immediately. An enjoyable class that any child would benefit from." – **Lisa Licano, Goddard School**

"Excellent Presentation!" – Ms. Hardin, Colina Elementary

*"Extremely appropriate and helpful." – **Ms. Tibbits, Desert Willow Elementary***

"Great for classroom management!"– Ms. Garrett, Stepping Stones Elementary

*"My students look forward to karate instruction every other Monday and it gives them motivation to stay disciplined during the school day!" – **Ms. Venafro, Stepping Stones Elementary***

*"Good manners in speaking to instructor" – **Molly Buchanan, Goddard School***

Thanks To The Contributors / Co-Authors!

Chief Master Patti Barnum

Chief Master Patti Barnum has over four decades of experience in education and martial arts and is the founder of **Success Now Martial Arts**. She's trained tens of thousands of students, instructors and Black Belts and continues to lead in her community and around the country. You can contact her for a consultation through **ATAStrong.com** or at her schools at:

Karate For Kids

7516 Cass Ave.	419 W. 55th St.
Darien, IL 60561	Countryside, IL 60525
630-271-1200	708-352-5323

Senior Master Laura Sanborn

Laura Sanborn is a 7° Black Belt, and the Chief of Staff for all KarateBuilt Martial Arts Schools. She is a specialist in instruction and program development as well as business training. You can contact her for a consultation or lessons at KarateBuilt.com or

KarateBuilt Martial Arts
29850 N. Tatum Blvd., Suite 105
Cave Creek AZ 85331
(480) 575-8171

Sarah Richards

Sarah Richards is a 1° Black Belt, technical and creative writing expert with a degree in creative writing from Arizona State University. She is available for writing, ghostwriting of all types and consultations on writing for fiction and non-fiction works. Contact at SarahWordsWeaver@gmail.com.

References

Note this is an *extended* set of references which includes my dissertation references (there are more than mentioned in the book) in case anyone decides they want to explore more.

Agatston, P. W., Kowalski, R., & Limber, S. (2007). Students' perspectives on cyber bullying. *The Journal of Adolescent Health : Official Publication of the Society for Adolescent Medicine*, *41*(6 Suppl 1), S59-60. doi:10.1016/j.jadohealth.2007.09.003

American Psychiatric Association. (2000). Diagnostic and statistical manual of mental disorders (4th ed., Text rev.). Washington, DC: Author.

American Psychological Association (APA). (n.d.). *Bullying* [Web page]. Retrieved from http://www.apa.org/topics/bullying/index.aspx

Anonymous. (2010, November 20). Bullying; total nonstop action TNA wrestling launches anti-bullying campaign. *Marketing Weekly News.*

Black, S., Washington, E., Trent, V., Harner, P., & Pollock, E. (2010). Translating the olweus bullying prevention program into real-world practice. *Health Promotion Practice*, *11*, 733-40. doi:10.1177/1524839908321562

Buhs, E. S., Ladd, G. W., & Herald, S. L. (2006). Peer exclusion and victimization: Processes that mediate the relation between peer group rejection and children's classroom engagement and achievement? *Journal of Educational Psychology, 98*, 1-13. doi:10.1037/0022-0663.98.1.1

Burrows, L. (2011). Don't try to bully gershon ben keren. *Jewish Advocate, 202*, 2.

Burt, I., & Butler, S. K. (2011). Capoeira as a clinical intervention: Addressing adolescent aggression with brazilian martial arts. *Journal of Multicultural Counseling and Development, 39*, 48-57. doi:10.1002/j.2161-1912.2011.tb00139.x

Byrne, B. J. (1994). Bullies and victims in a school setting with reference to some dublin schools. *Irish Journal of Psychology, 15*, 574-586.

Carr-Gregg, M., & Manocha, R. (2011). Bullying effects, prevalence and strategies for detection. *AUSTRALIAN FAMILY PHYSICIAN, 40*(3), 98-102.

Cheng, -Y., Chen, -M., Liu, -S., & Chen, -L. (2011). Development and psychometric evaluation of the school bullying scales: A Rasch measurement approach. *Educational and Psychological Measurement, 71*, 200-216. doi:10.1177/0013164410387387

Columbus, P. J., & Rice, D. (1998) Phenomenological meanings of martial arts participation. / Signification phenomenologique de la pratique des arts martiaux. *Journal of Sport Behavior, 21, 16-29.*

Craig, W., Pepler, D., & Blais, J. (2007). Responding to bullying: What works? *School Psychology International, 28*, 465-477. doi:10.1177/0143034307084136

Cunningham, P. B., Henggeler, S. W., Limber, S. P., Melton, G. B., & Nation, M. A. (2000). Patterns and correlates of gun ownership among nonmetropolitan and rural middle school students. *Journal of Clinical Child Psychology, 29*, 432-42. doi:10.1207/S15374424JCCP2903_14

Dussich, J. P., & Maekoya, C. (2007). Physical child harm and bullying-related behaviors: A comparative study in japan, south africa, and the united states. *International Journal of Offender Therapy and Comparative Criminology, 51*, 495-509. doi:10.1177/0306624X06298463

Eisenberg, M. E., Neumark-Sztainer, D., & Perry, C. L. (2003). Peer harassment, school connectedness, and academic achievement. *The Journal of School Health, 73*, 311-6.

Endresen, I. M., & Olweus, D. (2005a). Participation in power sports and antisocial involvement in preadolescent and adolescent boys. *Journal of Child Psychology and Psychiatry, and Allied Disciplines, 46*(5), 468-78. doi:10.1111/j.1469-7610.2005.00414.x

Endresen, I. M., & Olweus, D. (2005b). Participation in power sports and antisocial involvement in preadolescent and adolescent boys. *Journal of Child Psychology and Psychiatry, 46*, 468-478.

Fekkes, M., Pijpers, F. I., & Verloove-Vanhorick, S. P. (2004). Bullying behavior and associations with psychosomatic complaints and depression in victims. *The Journal of Pediatrics, 144*, 17-22. doi:10.1016/j.jpeds.2003.09.025

Fleming, L. C., & Jacobsen, K. H. (2009). Bullying and symptoms of depression in chilean middle school students. *The Journal of School Health, 79*, 130-137. doi:10.1111/j.1746-1561.2008.0397.x

Foster, Y. A. (1997). Brief aikido training versus karate and golf training and university students' scores on self-esteem, anxiety, and expression of anger. *Perceptual and Motor Skills, 84*, 609-10.

Frommer, D., & Angelove, K. (n.d.). One third of U.S. 11-Year-Olds have cellphones - business insider. *Business insider* [Web page]. Retrieved from http://articles.businessinsider.com/2010-01-19/tech/30037917_1_cellphones-mobile-phones-content

Gini, G., & Pozzoli, T. (2009). Association between bullying and psychosomatic problems: A meta-analysis. *Pediatrics, 123*, 1059-1065. doi:10.1542/peds.2008-1215

Glanz, J. (1994, May 15). A school/curricular intervention martial arts program for at-risk students. *ED375347.Pdf* [Paper Presented at the annual meeting of the safe schools coalition on "Gangs, Schools & Community" (2nd, Orlande FL, May 15th, 1994)] (Paper Presented at the annual meeting of the safe schools coalition on "Gangs, Schools & Community" (2nd, Orlande FL, May 15th, 1994)).

Hallford, A., Borntrager, C., & Davis, J. L. (2006). Evaluation of a bullying prevention program. *Journal of Research in Childhood Education, 21*, 91-101.

Haner, D., Pepler, D., Cummings, J., & Rubin-Vaughan, A. (2010). The role of arts-based curricula in bullying prevention: Elijah's kite--a children's opera. *Canadian Journal of School Psychology, 25*, 55-69. doi:10.1177/0829573509349031

It Ain't What You Don't Know That Gets You Into Trouble. It's What You Know for Sure That Just Ain't So . (2018, November 18). Retrieved from Quote Investigator: https://quoteinvestigator.com/2018/11/18/know-trouble/

Juvonen, J., Graham, S., & Schuster, M. A. (2003). Bullying among young adolescents: The strong, the weak, and the troubled. *Pediatrics, 112*, 1231-1237.

Kowalski, R. M., & Limber, S. P. (2007). Electronic bullying among middle school students. *The Journal of Adolescent Health : Official Publication of the Society for Adolescent Medicine, 41*(6 Suppl 1), S22-30. doi:10.1016/j.jadohealth.2007.08.017

Kumpulainen, K., & Räsänen, E. (2000). Children involved in bullying at elementary school age: Their psychiatric symptoms and deviance in adolescence. An epidemiological sample. *Child Abuse & Neglect, 24*, 1567-1577.

Kyriakides, L., Kaloyirou, C., & Lindsay, G. (2006). An analysis of the revised Olweus bully/victim questionnaire using the Rasch measurement model. *The British Journal of Educational Psychology, 76*, 781-801. doi:10.1348/000709905X53499

Lai, S. L., Ye, R. M., & Chang, K. P. (2008). Bullying in middle schools: An asian-pacific regional study. *ASIA PACIFIC EDUCATION REVIEW, 9*(4), 503-+.

Layton, C. (1988). The personality of black-belt and nonblack-belt traditional karateka. Perceptual and Motor Skills, 67, 218.

Lee, H. U. (1993a). *The way of traditional taekwondo volume A: Philosophy and tradition.* Little Rock, AR: American Taekwondo Association.

Lee, H. U. (1993b). *The way of traditional taekwondo volume one: White belt.* Little Rock, AR: American Taekwondo Association.

Lee, J. (n.d.). *President obama & the first lady at the white house conference on bullying prevention | the white house* [Web page]. Retrieved from http://www.whitehouse.gov/blog/2011/03/10/pre sident-obama-first-lady-white-house-conference-bullying-prevention

Lee Duckworth, A., Steen, T. A., & Seligman, M. E. (2005). Positive psychology in clinical practice. *Annual Review of Clinical Psychology, 1,* 629-651. doi:10.1146/annurev.clinpsy.1.102803.144154

Lee, T. H., Cornell, D. G., & Cole, J. C. (n.d.). Concurrent validity of the Olweus bully/victim questionnaire, *Virginia Youth Violence Project.*

McDonald. (2007, May 4). One special sensei - mike cherwaty has a way of bringing out the best in his martial arts students, including a 15-year-old boy with autism. *Niagara This Week.*

Mooij T. National campaign effects on secondary pupils' bullying and violence. Br J Educ Psychol. 2005 Sep;75(Pt 3):489-511. doi: 10.1348/000709904X23727. PMID: 16238878.

Nansel, T. R., Craig, W., Overpeck, M. D., Saluja, G., & Ruan, W. J. (2004). Cross-national consistency in the relationship between bullying behaviors and psychosocial adjustment. *Archives of Pediatrics & Adolescent Medicine, 158*, 730-736. doi:10.1001/archpedi.158.8.730

Nansel, T. R., Overpeck, M., Pilla, R. S., Ruan, W. J., Simmons-Morton, B., & Scheidt, P. (2001). Bullying behaviors among US youth prevalence and association with psychosocial adjustment. *Journal of the American Medical Association, 285*, 2094-2100.

Olweus, D. (1993). Bullying at school: What we know and what we can do. Cambridge: Blackwell.

Olweus, D., & Limber, S. P. (2007). *Olweus bullying prevention program : Teacher guide*. Center City, MN: Hazelden.

Olweus, D., & Limber, S. P. (2010a). Bullying in school: Evaluation and dissemination of the olweus bullying prevention program. *The American Journal of Orthopsychiatry, 80*, 124-134. doi:10.1111/j.1939-0025.2010.01015.x

Olweus, D., & Limber, S. P. (2010, November 17). What we are learning about bullying. *Meeting of the international bullying prevention association*.

Prince, D. S. (1996). Self-concept in martial arts students. In <u>*Dissertation abstracts international: Section B: The sciences and engineering*</u> [Dissertation Abstracts International: Section B: The Sciences and Engineering] (p. 1451).

Rawana, . S., Norwood, . J., & Whitley, J. (2011). A mixed-method evaluation of a strength-based bullying prevention program. *Canadian Journal of School Psychology, 26,* 283-300. doi:10.1177/0829573511423741

Rigby, K., & Smith, P. K. (2011). Is school bullying really on the rise? *Social Psychology of Education, 14,* 441-455. doi:10.1007/s11218-011-9158-y

Rindfleisch, T. (2010, December 15). UW-L study: Martial arts benefit autistic kids. *LaCrosse Tribune,*

Rock, E. A., Hammond, M., & Rasmussen, S. (2007). School-Wide bullying prevention program for elementary students. *Journal of Emotional Abuse, 4,* 225-239. doi:10.1300/J135v04n03_13

Rodelli, M., De Bourdeaudhuij, I., Dumon, E., Portzky, G., & DeSmet, A. (2018). Which healthy lifestyle factors are associated with a lower risk of suicidal ideation among adolescents faced with cyberbullying?. *Preventive medicine, 113,* 32–40. https://doi.org/10.1016/j.ypmed.2018.05.002

(Davis, 2017) (Brown, 2010) (Davis, 2017; Olweus Bullying Prevention Program, n.d.)Roland, E. (2011). The broken curve: Effects of the norwegian manifesto against bullying. *International Journal of Behavioral Development, 35,* 383-388. doi:10.1177/0165025411407454

Ross, S. W., & Horner, R. H. (2009). Bully prevention in positive behavior support. *Journal of Applied Behavior Analysis, 42,* 747-759. doi:10.1901/jaba.2009.42-747

Salin, D. (2010). Prevalence and forms of bullying among business professionals: A comparison of two different strategies for measuring bullying. *European Journal of Work and Organizational Psychology*, 425-441.

Sayer, D. (2008, March 6). Course will teach kids self-defense techniques - the goal of the program is to help children learn how to escape an attacker and how to deal with bullies. *Portland Press Herald.*

Schvey, N. A., Marwitz, S. E., Mi, S. J., Galescu, O. A., Broadney, M. M., Young-Hyman, D., Brady, S. M., Reynolds, J. C., Tanofsky-Kraff, M., Yanovski, S. Z., & Yanovski, J. A. (2019). Weight-based teasing is associated with gain in BMI and fat mass among children and adolescents at-risk for obesity: A longitudinal study. *Pediatric Obesity, 14*(10), e12538. https://doi.org/10.1111/ijpo.12538

Stableford, D., 'Scary Guy' with facial tattoos paid $6,500 a day to teach kids to stop bullying. [Web page]. Retrieved from https://news.yahoo.com/blogs/sideshow/scary-guy-facial-tattoos-paid-6-500-day-194040510.html

Stuart-Cassel, V., Bell, A., & Springer, J. F. (2011). Analysis of state bullying laws and policies. *Office of Planning, Evaluation and Policy Development, US Department of Education*, 202.

The Full History Of ATA International. [Web page]. Retrieved from https://www.atamartialarts.com/about/full-ata-international-history/

Tomic-Latinac, M., & Nikcevic-Milkovic, A. (2009). Evaluation of UNICEF bullying prevention programme efficiency. *LJETOPIS SOCIJALNOG RADA, 16,* 635-657.

Trost, S. G., Pate, R. R., Sallis, J. F., Freedson, P. S., Taylor, W. C., Dowda, M., & Sirard, J. (2002). Age and gender differences in objectively measured physical activity in youth. *Medicine and Science in Sports and Exercise, 34,* 350-355.

Twemlow, S. W., & Sacco, F. C. (1998). The application of traditional martial arts practice and theory to the treatment of violent adolescents. *Adolescence, 33,* 505-519.

Twemlow, S. W., Sacco, F. C., & Fonagy, P. (2008). Embodying the mind: Movement as a container for destructive aggression. *American Journal of Psychotherapy, 62,* 1-33.

Urban, P. (1993). *The karate dojo: Traditions and tales of the martial arts.* Tokyo: Charles E. Tuttle Publishing Co.

van der Wal, M. F., de Wit, C. A., & Hirasing, R. A. (2003). Psychosocial health among young victims and offenders of direct and indirect bullying. *Pediatrics, 111*(6 Pt 1), 1312-1317.

Waasdorp, T. E., Bradshaw, C. P., & Leaf, P. J. (2012). The impact of schoolwide positive behavioral interventions and supports on bullying and peer rejection: A randomized controlled effectiveness trial. *Archives of Pediatrics & Adolescent Medicine, 166,* 149-156. doi:10.1001/archpediatrics.2011.755

Wade, A., & Beran, T. (2011). Cyberbullying: The new era of bullying. *Canadian Journal of School Psychology*, *26*, 44-61. doi:10.1177/0829573510396318

Zivin, G., Hassan, N. R., DePaula, G. F., Monti, D. A., Harlan, C., Hossain, K. D., & Patterson, K. (2001). An effective approach to violence prevention: Traditional martial arts in middle school. *Adolescence*, *36*, 443-459.

Highly Recommended TED Talks:

Brown, B. (2010, June). *The power of vulnerability*. Retrieved from TED.com: https://www.ted.com/talks/brene_brown_the_power_of_vulnerability

Bosler, A., & Greene, D. (2017, February). *How to practice effectively...for just about anything*. Retrieved from https://www.ted.com/talks/annie_bosler_and_don_greene_how_to_practice_effectively_for_just_about_anything

Davis, D. (2017, November). *Why I, as a black man, attend KKK rallies*. Retrieved from TED.com: https://www.ted.com/talks/daryl_davis_why_i_as_a_black_man_attend_kkk_rallies

Sources on Bullying

Olweus Bullying Prevention Program. (n.d.). Retrieved from Olweus Bullying Prevention Program: https://clemsonolweus.org

PACER's National Bullying Prevention Center. (n.d.). Retrieved 12 31, 2023, from Pacer.org: http://www.pacer.org/bullying/

StopBullying.gov. (n.d.). Retrieved 12 31, 2023, from U.S. Department of Health & Human Services: http://www.stopbullying.gov

We Also Get Asked About Getting Started in Martial Arts at KarateBuilt...

Founded in 1995 by Dr. Greg Moody, an 8th degree Black Belt and Chief Master Instructor, KarateBuilt Martial Arts and Karate lessons for pre-school children ages 3-6 and elementary age kids ages 7 and up are designed to develop the critical building blocks kids need – specialized for their age group – for school excellence and later success in life.

KarateBuilt Martial Arts Adult Karate training is a complete adult fitness and conditioning program for adults who want to lose weight, get (and stay in shape), or learn self-defense in a supportive environment.

Instructors can answer questions or be contacted 24 hours of the day, 7 days a week at 866-311-1032 for one of our nationwide locations. You can also visit our website at KarateBuilt.com.

About **Dr. Greg Moody**: Greg is an 8th degree Black Belt and Chief Master Instructor. He has a Ph.D. in Special Education from Arizona State University (along with a Master's Degree in Counseling and a Bachelor's Degree in Engineering – *he actually is a rocket scientist*). Chief Master Moody is a motivational speaker and educator and teaches seminars in bullying, business, and martial arts training, around the world. **See more at** DrGregMoody.com.

The KarateBuilt Martial Arts Headquarters is in Cave Creek, Arizona at 29850 N. Tatum Blvd., Suite 105, Cave Creek AZ 85331. You can locate the Chief Instructor, Master Laura Sanborn there directly at (480) 575-8171.

If You Would Like To Work With Dr. Greg Moody, Master Instructor

There are a variety of ways to work with Dr. Moody on a limited basis.

For speaking (including keynote speaking and training) and seminars. To schedule with him, email Greg@DrGregMoody.com and provide:

- Full contact information for all representatives

- Topic (in detail)

- Your organization's complete information and structure

For consulting. To schedule with him, email Greg@DrGregMoody.com and provide:

- Full contact information for all representatives

- Scope of work, including key goals and metrics

- Your organization's complete information and structure

c

Made in United States
Orlando, FL
03 April 2024

45417134R00164